Hemingway's Cuban Son

HEMINGWAY'S CUBAN SON

Reflections on the Writer by His Longtime Majordomo

René Villarreal & Raúl Villarreal

The Kent State University Press
Kent, Ohio

Library of Congress Catalog Card Number 2008040889
ISBN 978-0-87338-977-8
Manufactured in the United States of America

All photos, unless otherwise noted, are from the Villarreal Family Collection.

Library of Congress Cataloging-in-Publication Data
Villarreal, René, 1929–
Hemingway's Cuban son : reflections on the writer by his longtime Majordomo / by Rene Villarreal and Raul Villarreal.
p. cm.
ISBN 978-0-87338-977-8 (alk. paper) ∞
1. Hemingway, Ernest, 1899–1961—Homes and haunts—Cuba—Havana.
2. Hemingway, Ernest, 1899–1961—Friends and associates.
3. Authors, American—20th century—Biography.
4. Americans—Cuba—Biography.
I. Martínez, Raúl, 1964– II. Title.
PS3515.E37Z914 2009
813'.52—dc22
[B]
2008040889

British Library Cataloging-in-Publication data are available.

13 12 11 10 09 5 4 3 2 1

In loving memory of

Rodolfo Emilio Villarreal

PREFACE

> *He was stiff and sore now and his wounds and all of the strained parts of his body hurt with the cold of the night. I hope I do not have to fight again, he thought. I hope so much I do not have to fight again.*
>
> —Ernest Hemingway, *The Old Man and the Sea*

My father, René Villarreal, first wrote his memoirs in the mid-1960s when he was serving as the director and administrator of the Hemingway Museum in Havana, Cuba. However, that manuscript was either lost or stolen—we're not sure which, because those involved and the events that followed remain vague and elusive to this day. It wasn't until the summer of 1996, at the age of sixty-six, that my father agreed to rewrite his memoirs. But his mindset was different then, following the sudden death of a son. As he mourned in silence, he read his favorite work by Ernest Hemingway, *The Old Man and the Sea,* a book he has turned to at different stages in his life. The story of the old Cuban fisherman took on new meaning for him. He identified with Santiago's struggle against the big fish and the loss of the fish to the sharks. But it was not a brother he had lost, as Santiago refers to the big fish in the novella; it was a son. Certain passages in *The Old Man and the Sea* gave my father the strength and determination to begin and complete this project. Some years later, and dealing with numerous health issues, the old man is tired but still alive with lucid memories of his life at the Finca Vigía.

Although I was not born until 1964, I grew up with Hemingway. As a young child, I visited the Finca Vigía in the afternoons with my two older brothers, quietly observing our father guide tour after tour and observe visitors take pictures of him, shake his hand, and ask for autographs. Throughout our house in San Francisco de Paula, just a few blocks from the Finca, Papa Hemingway was present—in photographs, books, and letters. And there were the wonderful stories my father and others in our small village told.

We left Cuba in 1972 for Madrid, Spain. Life there was very different from what we had known, but we assimilated and settled into a good and happy life. During the 1970s other families settled in the surrounding neighborhoods, and a small Cuban community formed. However, in 1974, with the changing political climate in Spain, my father moved the family to the United States, where we settled in Union City, New Jersey, once referred to as "Havana on the Hudson" because of its large population of Cuban exiles (second only to Miami, Florida).

I never discussed with my father why he remained quiet on the subject of Ernest Hemingway in public and refused to give any interviews after 1973. For decades he was sought after for interviews, and for years rumors of his whereabouts placed him in Florida, Costa Rica, Canada, and even back in Cuba. I thought he simply wanted to put the memories of life at the Finca Vigía and Hemingway behind him. Perhaps, I thought, deep inside it hurt him to talk about those years.

But after my brother's death, I began to ask my father more questions. I must have sensed his need to reconsider the past. Or maybe I, the youngest son, needed to pull him out of grief and back to us. And so during that summer of 1996, I began interviewing him. Over the course of two years, usually on weekends, we sat down and shared a glass of good Spanish wine and Montecristos, our favorite Cuban cigars. I clicked on the tape recorder and asked a question or two. It took nothing more for the stories I had listened to throughout my childhood to flow out, richly detailed and descriptive, something much more than mere anecdotes or musings. Those insighful accounts of his life at the Finca Vigía offered a unique perspective on a man known for his writing as well as his passion. My father's is a story very different from what others have written about Ernest Hemingway.

This memoir shines light on Hemingway's life in Cuba—his working habits, his state of mind, and his love for the island and its people. We do not intend to defend or criticize the man but to detail the events of the time and the place as my father perceived and remembered them.

Also, this is a book about my father's childhood and young manhood, about his home, his land. It is an account of two very different lives connected by a chance encounter in 1939.

My father has the gifts of a keen memory and artful storytelling, a great Cuban tradition that was surely sharpened and honed during his years with Papa Hemingway. He closes his eyes and relives the scenes with great detail, with all of his senses, with his whole being. I found very little discrepency between the interview recordings and what he wrote down with pencil and paper. He recalled names and dates immediately and accurately. In researching biographical details, I checked dates and names against reputable biographies. When I found discrepencies between my father's memory and the texts, I pressed him for even more details and points of references, which he delivered without hesitation, maintaining his original statements and date. He proved to be my most consistently reliable source.

In working with my father in writing this memoir, I came to better understand him, to more fully appreciate and respect his life. He entrusted me with his treasured accounts of his life at the Finca Vigía, and I wanted his story to be told with his voice and through his eyes. The stories are not from any single interview or translation. Rather, they grow out of all the material I have gathered from my father and researched myself. It was a difficult task selecting from so many wonderful stories which ones would best tell his story, which would best represent his life.

Helping me to understand that time in my father's life, that world, were the many photographs in my family's possesion. A few my father had well before Papa's death; most Mary Hemingway gave him before burning the others. Sadly, many, many more—pictures of my father boxing with Papa, playing baseball, feeding the cats—were lost in Cuba, along with the manuscript and other personal items. The images that now make up the Villarreal Family Collection were scattered among family members in Cuba and slowly, painstakingly recovered. Where photographers' names were listed or known, I received permission from survivors to reprint here. I received permission from the estates of George Leavans and Earl Theisen, who beautifully photographed Hemingway's life in Cuba.

This is the story of a poor, young Cuban boy who grew into a man and gained the trust, respect, and love of a famous American writer, a man he called Papa.

RAÚL VILLARREAL

ACKNOWLEDGMENTS

To my father, I extend my sincere gratitude, love, and great admiration for sharing his incredible life with me and for recognizing that his youngest son is a dreamer. My soul-felt gratitude to my mother for her love and strength throughout the years and to my brother René Jr., my dear sisters Fanny and Martha, and all my nieces and nephews.

My father and I extend our immense appreciation to Sandra Spanier for coming into our lives and being such a great friend to us and also the Villarreal family in Cuba. Also, many thanks to the following individuals for their wonderful friendship and support throughout this project: Larry Grimes, DeWitt Sage, John Mullholland, Michael Smith, Jack Thornton, Andrea Herrera O'Reilly, Lourdes Gil, Iraida Iturralde, Maritza Bolaños, Gladys Rodríguez Ferrero, and Ada Rosa Alfonso Rosales.

We will forever be grateful to my agent, Mary Yost, who always kept the faith. We extend our gratitude, love, and admiration to Joanna Hildebrand Craig, the best editor anyone could ever hope for. She believed in this project from the start, providing me with great insightful comments and suggestions in order to make sure this was the best, most honest book it could be.

Finally, I must thank my beautiful and adventurous wife, Rita, for her neverending love and support and for sharing the madness with me for all these wonderful years.

RAÚL VILLARREAL

CUBA 1996

Fours years had passed since my last trip to Cuba, and I thought this one would be my last. This trip was supposed to give me the opportunity to say good-bye, to see my brothers, sister, and old friends one last time. I wanted to see Cuba once more. I wanted to see again the place where I had lived the best years of my life. Even in exile, I always considered Cuba my home.

In the years since I was last there, life had fundamentally changed. I lost a son. I became a changed man, hollow, empty. The pain of losing Rodolfo a couple of months after his thirty-sixth birthday was too much to endure. Even though I had a wonderful wife, four loving children, and eight beautiful grandchildren, I could hardly stand the pain. I had lost my desire to live. I would have offered my life a thousand times for his, but life betrayed me. A lifetime ago Fanny, my dear wife, and I had to endure the loss of another child, a son who died just days after he was born. It was very painful then, but we were young and full of life. Five more children were born afterward to help us with our loss. But we lost Rodolfo after seeing him become a man.

Fanny found comfort in the constant love and attention from the kids and grandchildren, but I still saw the hurt in her eyes. I found no comfort, not in anything. I love all my children dearly, but Rodolfo had a special place in my heart. He reminded me of my oldest brother, Heliodoro. Rodolfo was charismatic, full of life, adventurous, and he had a mischievious streak that captured my heart.

I was blessed with a beautiful family. René Jr. turned out to be the responsible, serious, "father" type, often looking after his younger siblings. Fanny, the oldest of the girls, named after her mother, is quiet, sweet, and very protective. Martha, the youngest, is the independent career woman who solves the family's problems. Raúl, the youngest of the boys, is the artist. My family always makes me proud. Fanny and I raised them well. We tried to teach them right from wrong, to teach them all we could, to raise them the same way our parents raised us. I realized how fortunate my life had been. I had a wonderful family, a good decent life, and the privilege of knowing one of the great American writers of the twentieth century. I had been Ernest Hemingway's friend—su hombre de confianza, his right-hand man, su hijo cubano.

The children urged us to make the trip to Cuba, hoping it would help after Rodolfo's death. Raúl said he would accompany us. He didn't want us to travel alone. His brother and sisters made him promise he would take good care of us. I invited Rosa Santurces to join us on the trip. Though a distant relative by marriage, most of my family referred to her as Aunt Rosa. She had left Cuba in 1968. She was now eighty-four years old, twice widowed, and very independent. She had refused to move to Miami, Florida, with her blood relatives and lived alone in a small apartment in New York City. At her age, she was happy to be going home once more.

We left from Kennedy Airport early on the morning of Friday, May 10, 1996, landing in Nassau close to noon. As the passengers destined for Cuba entered the terminal, the band that had been playing island music started to play *La Guantanamera.* I felt a rush of emotion and understood why I was making this trip. Most of the passengers were like me—Cubans returning home—and we all sat together in the hot, humid airport terminal waiting for the connecting flight to Havana. I studied the faces of my fellow passengers, looking to distingish between the non-Cubans traveling for pleasure and Cubans traveling to visit family. Those of us visiting family all had the same look of worry, anticipation, uncertainty. We had worked hard all year to save money for this trip, to buy clothes, shoes, eyeglasses, toys—anything a family member had asked for in a letter or over the phone. But we now wondered what to expect when the bags are weighed, how much money it would take to get the luggage through. And we were nervous because we didn't know how customs would treat us, how long it would take before we saw our loved ones, what we would find when we got there.

Sitting there among my own, I had renewed appreciation for the strength and beauty of the Cuban people. Most of the passengers were my age. The few young passengers, wide-eyed and eager, were probably visiting Cuba for the first time, traveling with their parents to finally meet a cousin, aunt, or uncle they had only seen in photographs, known through correspondence, or spoken with on the telephone. Respect and love for family has kept all of us together, even across great distances and through difficult times. Fanny and I work all year without taking vacations, saving every penny in order to make this trip and spend two weeks with our family and childhood friends. The sacrifices are worth it, for we know that in these two weeks we can forget about our aches and troubles and remember the old days and good times. These short weeks warm our hearts until the next time we visit.

I looked at Fanny. I saw the sadness in her eyes. It was two days before Mother's Day. I caught her glance and smiled. She smiled back and asked if I had my heart pills at hand. That was the third time she had asked me. I showed her the pill bottle again, and she nodded. Five months had passed since our son's death, and we still walked in a trance of disbelief. Fanny is a strong woman. I was blessed when I met her. I love her now more than ever.

Raúl scratched his head as he walked around our luggage and smiled at us. He was only seven when we left Cuba, but he remembers quite a lot. We knew we couldn't have made the trip without him. He took care of all the details at the airports, completing all the paperwork, bringing cold drinks when we were thirsty, and taking care of our luggage. God knows there was a lot of luggage! He was very excited about bringing back my manuscripts and starting work on the memoir. I planned to give him the manuscript, the photographs, and my blessing. I knew I couldn't commit myself to writing a book.

We waited hours for the plane to arrive from Cuba. Finally, at a little past three in the afternoon, we were ready to board. Three lines formed at the weigh-in counter. Even after the wait and the heat, there were no arguments or even much impatience among the passengers. After all, most of us had spent countless hours of our lives waiting in long lines for rations and to have the libretas stamped, one for clothes and shoes and the other for milk, meat, rice, beans, oil, or soap. Once everyone had checked their luggage and payed the excess baggage fees—we were allowed 44 pounds of checked luggage, but most of us had over 80 pounds' worth—we boarded the small Aerolinea Cubana airplane and, without much preflight preparation from the crew, took off.

The start of the flight was entertaining. After quickly dispensing with the safety instructions, the flight attendants became mile-high flea market merchants, peddling bottles of dark and light Havana Club Rum, Montecristo and Cohiba cigars, Marlboro and Salem cigarettes, Alicia Alonso perfume, and audiotapes of recent Cuban hits. The rum, cigars, cigarettes, and music were the best sellers; no one asked for the Alicia Alonso fragrance. We passengers enjoyed ourselves and relaxed, drinking Cuba libres or, as some quietly called them, mentiritas, which means "little lie." There was much laughing and stories told about family members they were visiting. I overheard a businessman tell the man sitting next to him of a place in Havana where he could have the best massage in the world for only ten American dollars. He could have the "full treatment," and it would be "out of this world." He advised his friend that no matter how satisfied he would be, he was not to pay more than ten dollars.

I settled into my own reverie. I thought of Cuba, my childhood, my family and friends, my life at the Finca Vigía with Papa Hemingway, and then Rodolfo. As much as I tried, I could not help but think of him.

In under an hour's time, the plane began its descent. I watched out the window as the clouds gave way to the beautiful terra-cotta earth and emerald-green vegetation. My heart pounded. Fanny gently told me to place a heart pill under my tongue. With a thrilling bump and a cheer in the cabin, we landed in José Martí International airport, the very same airport I had left Cuba from with my wife and five children in 1972. Ignoring instructions, most of the excited passengers were out of their seats, retrieving their carry-on bags, and securing their rum and cigarettes well before the plane came to a complete stop.

When I stepped out of the plane onto the tarmac, I felt the warm Cuban breeze gently caress my face. With a deep breath, I took it all in. The sweet smell of mi Cuba. How I had missed it!

Three long, red buses took us passengers and our luggage to the customs office. There, we got off the bus and walked inside the building. Raúl carried most of the luggage, with me and Fanny seeing to our carry-on bags and one large suitcase with wheels. Raúl told us to wait with the luggage and went to talk to a customs agent about our entry visas. Our visas had not arrived in the United States on time, so we had been instructed by our travel agent to retrieve them at the customs office in Cuba. In a few minutes, Raúl returned holding our visas. I saw the look of relief on his face. I was relieved myself, because when traveling to Cuba you never know what problems or complications may surface. We gathered ourselves and all our bags and went to the customs room.

We were happy to learn that a family member who held a job in the airport had saved our luggage from a search and made sure we weren't charged excess weight fees. But we were not spared the security check. Fanny, who had in her carry-on the oil paint set Raúl was taking to my brother Oscar, was stopped by one of the customs agents. The paint tubes and palette knives must have looked suspicious in the antiquated X-ray machine. Opening the wooden case, the agent saw twelve sets of oil colors, several painting brushes, and palette knives. Nervously, I tried to hand the man twenty American dollars so he would leave my wife alone. Raúl told me to put the money away. He explained to the man that the oil set was a present for his uncle. There was no doubt the man had his eye on the paint set. Perhaps he had a relative who was an artist and wished to get the set for him, or perhaps he wanted to sell it on the street. He could live half a year on the money he would get for it on the black market. At that moment, our cousin came over and persuaded the customs agent to leave us alone. Then we were free to proceed. It had only taken a short fifteen minutes. I remember previous visits when we had been detained in customs for well over two hours.

Three porters came with carts to relieve us of the bags. Raúl carried a large bag and walked behind all of us, making sure the porters didn't take anything. As we walked out, I looked back. The rest of the passengers were going through the degrading procedure of having to bargain and haggle for the belongings in their luggage. I felt bad, wishing I could somehow help, but I knew there was nothing I could do.

We walked out of the noisy and crowded terminal. I heard my sister's voice calling out to me. I heard other voices calling out to us. I looked around and finally saw Nilda, my sister, and her oldest daughter, Elvira. Then I saw my two brothers Luis and Oscar. Every time we visited, the family somehow managed to provide transportation—but certainly at great expense. People who owned cars made more money driving tourists around than working in their profession, even engineers or doctors.

Twelve family members were there to greet us. The affection was overwhelming. We spent a full fifteen minutes just hugging and kissing. I looked at my sister and tears welled in my eyes. She squeezed my hand and whispered, "Aqui no," not here. My twin brother, Luis, cried when we looked into each other's eyes. He had lost his youngest son almost ten years ago in a train accident. He knew what I was going through.

When the hugs were shared and the initial greetings were said, we all got into the four hired cars—all of them big old American "classic" cars that seemed to belong to an era long gone—and headed to San Francisco de Paula, the village that was my family's home.

From the airport we took the road to Rancho Boyeros. For me, the busy, happy chatter receded into the background as I looked out the window. It was late in the afternoon, but the sun had not gone down yet. The day was still bright. Along the bumpy, dusty road were young and old folk alike riding bicycles or waiting to be picked up by a good samaritan with a truck or car. I saw a man wearing a straw hat riding a horse bareback, a shirtless barefooted child riding behind, holding tightly to his father's waist. The boy's hair was covered with dust. This was my Cuba—the Cuba of men on horses, of fiestas and serenatas, of a simpler, slower way of life. I knew that many things had changed in Cuba, but much remained the same.

In no time we were driving west past El Cotorro via La Carretera Central, and I could see the first hints of capitalism in this village just east of San Francisco de Paula. Cafes and grocery stores stood along the side of the road. They had not been there on my last trip. I looked for paladares but saw none. A successful paladar, a private home that opened its dining rooms to tourists and locals who paid for the homey fare, could have a regular clientele and make a decent living for the family.

We passed the old Cerveceria Hatuey factory, which meant we were getting closer to San Francisco de Paula. And in no time we turned off the highway and entered my old hometown. Here, little had changed over the last four years. San Francisco de Paula had remained a simple, humble, and poor town. On a little hilltop overlooking town, a sign read "Reparto la Prosperidad," but prosperity had not reached San Francisco de Paula.

The side road was in worse condition than the main highway, and our driver had a difficult time maneuvering around the large ditches and rocks. He drove slowly to avoid the large holes in the road. People stopped to watch the parade of cars—people from the pueblo, people I knew. They recognized me and waved. They knew we were coming. Like in every small town, word gets out fast.

We arrived at Nilda's house and were among family. Raúl allowed his uncles and cousins to carry the bags. In the welcoming, modest house, I sat down on a chair by the door and sighed in relief. Raúl, with new energy, walked around greeting people. Nilda told the drivers that she would take care of them later and they left. One of my nieces brought me cold bottled water. I had gotten sick on the last trip when I drank the water from the faucet, so they had bought bottled water. The money I sent every two months helped my family get through the rough times, and they more than paid us back on our visits.

"I missed you so much," I said to Nilda when she returned from the kitchen with café for Fanny and Aunt Rosa.

"I missed you too." She started to cry.

"I wanted to see you one last time before . . ." I hesitated, now sobbing. Fanny cried too. The room grew quiet.

"I didn't come all the way here to have you both crying! You could have stayed in Jersey for that!" Raúl scolded, upset. "I wanted you to be happy. Don't start talking nonsense!"

Raúl had never spoken to us like that before, but he knew it was the only way to snap me out of my gloomy frame of mind. My sister and brothers agreed; they didn't want the visit to turn into twelve days of mourning. Raúl was right. We had not come to Cuba to cry.

And soon I did feel better. I watched Fanny smile and laugh as she talked to her sisters and nieces. Aunt Rosa forgot the aches and pains of old age. We talked late into the night telling them about the children and grandchildren, about their jobs and our lives. We talked about Rodolfo and other family members who had passed away. Raúl and I told them about our plans to write a book about my time with Papa Hemingway, news that was met with cheers. I knew that they all thought I should have done it long ago. I had only agreed to it now because Raúl would see the project through to completion. More importantly, I knew that he would never twist my words or make up lies the way others who have interviewed me have done through the years.

We talked and reminisced until we could no longer keep our eyes open. My sister had made sleeping arrangements for us in the house. (Aunt Rosa went to stay with relatives in El Cotorro.) We never stayed in a hotel. That was unthinkable. It meant inconveniences, but no one minded. Raúl took the small middle bedroom. Fanny and I slept in the larger bedroom at the front of the house. My sister, her husband, two of their daughters, and their husbands slept in the third, and largest, bedroom at the rear of the house. I knew it was a big sacrifice on their part, but they wouldn't have it any other way.

As we settled into bed, the warm breeze carried the sweet scent of mi Cuba into the bedroom. That night, back home among family, I slept better than I had in five months.

After a few days of rest, my brothers, Raúl, and I went to the Finca Vigía, the estate that was once the home of Ernest Hemingway—the place where I had worked since childhood, the place where I grew from a boy into a man. This was my other home. The Finca had been donated to the Cuban people by Mary Welsh Hemingway in 1961 and been designated a museum by the Cuban government. In December 1979, the first year the Cuban government allowed exiles who had family to visit the island, Fanny, Raúl, and I spent a week in Cuba, but I was not allowed to visit the Finca. It was not until my visit in 1983 that I was invited to step onto the Finca grounds again, after fifteen years away.

Carlito, a friend of the family, drove us there in his orange VW beetle, a vehicle he maintained with spare parts from a different array of cars. (Carlito had been a mechanical engineer, but now he made more money driving tourists around Havana.) We drove up to the large white gate at the front of the property. Two teenage girls dressed in school uniforms sitting inside a white wooden booth confirmed who we were and waved us in with warm smiles. We drove up the road and parked by the garage. The director of the museum arranged to meet us in what used to be the garage and which now served as an exhibition space. After formal greetings, we sat and spoke for a few minutes before beginning a tour of the estate.

I could see the excitement in Raúl's eyes. During the years I worked as administrator of the museum, from 1962 to 1968, my sons regularly visited me after school. They played and roamed around the Finca as if it was their own home. Raúl was not yet in school, so sometimes I took him with me after lunch, carrying him on my shoulders all the way up to the house. My eyes and legs were better then. He remembers all of that. But then, the Finca is a hard place to forget.

We left the garage and headed to the main house, walking up the terraced concrete steps. Right off I noticed a smaller ceiba tree in the place where a large, old ceiba used to be. It had been Papa's favorite tree. The director told me it had been cut down because the tree's branches were damaging the roof and its roots pushing up the floor tiles inside the house.

We entered through the front door and met several of the employees, all women. Outside, peering through the windows, several tourists stared at us, clearly wondering why we had been allowed inside (most visitors are only allowed to look into the house through the windows). We walked from room to room, and the museum director asked me questions, pencil and notepad in hand. I felt at home and glad to be there. I answered her questions without having to force my mind. I caught Raúl smiling at me. I knew he was proud of my memory, as was I.

In the Venetian Room, the guest room, Raúl photographed me and my brothers standing under the portrait of Papa Hemingway that my younger brother, Oscar, had painted in the late 1940s. It had been many years since the three of us stood inside this house together. We also took pictures under the massive buffalo trophy on the wall. All the while the curious, nosey tourists followed us, straining to hear our conversation through the windows. I heard one say loudly, "That's Hemingway's Cuban son" and felt a quick flush of pride.

From the dining room we went out to the terrace. I discreetly pointed out to Raúl only where the cats' cemetery was. Papa had always wanted the cat cemetery to remain a secret. We walked over to the white tower building that was completed in 1949 to see a photography exhibit entitled "Hemingway in Venice," which featured large black-and-white shots of Hemingway and his fourth wife, Mary Welsh, in Venice in 1948. As we left the tower, several tourists approached and asked me to autograph their exhibit pamphlets. The last was a young Cuban man who wasn't concerned at all about the rain that had started to fall. After I signed his pamphlet, he thanked me several times, shaking my hand vigorously. I was surprised that people still remembered who I was. I thought that, after so many years living outside Cuba, my connection to Papa Hemingway would have been forgotten.

Back inside the garage, the director asked me more questions, specifically regarding Papa Hemingway's daily routine of recording his weight and writing down comments on his bathroom walls. She took notes.

The rain finally stopped, and it was time to go. Before leaving, the director asked us all to sign the guest book. Carlito, our driver, had been with us the whole time, and as he signed the book, on his face I saw the great joy and pride of being part of this exclusive tour. I was the last one to sign. The Finca had been my home, and it felt strange signing the book. For many years I witnessed guest after guest sign the book, and now my signature was among them. How many names were in that book!

During the years I worked for Ernest Hemingway, I met many famous people. The Finca Vigía hosted visitors from all over the world. After Papa's death, I became director of the museum, and then I met many other great writers, such as Camilo José Cela, Alberto Moravia, and Alejo Carpentier, who extended their hands to me in friendship. In 1965 I had the pleasure of meeting and spending the afternoon with Cuban artist Wifredo Lam, drinking rum under the giant ceiba tree.

I was glad the government had tried to keep things as I left them. They still had Hemingway's yacht, the *Pilar*, on display by the pool, his typewriter and reading glasses in his bedroom, and the hunting trophies throughout the house. During the years I worked as administrator of the museum, I spoke to thousands of people who admired Ernest Hemingway, the man and his work. With great interest, they listened to my stories and anecdotes, to my lists of his likes and dislikes, to my chronicling of day-in-day-out activities. While I described many details of Papa's life in Cuba, many more stories and anecdotes I kept to myself, the memories too personal and meaningful to share with the too curious or with reporters or biographers. It was a job I loved.

Standing on the grounds of this familiar place, enjoying the scent of orchid trees, hibiscus, and jasmin trumpets, brought back many memories of the happy times of my life alongside Papa Hemingway. But it also brought back some of the bitterness over why I left.

In the late 1960s, the Ministry of National Culture started to make my life difficult because I shied away from joining any one political group. El Ministerio Nacional de Cultura refused to accept my noninvolvement. By 1968 the situation had become unbearable. The constant spying on me and my family as well as the lack of proper materials and trained personnel to maintain the museum forced me to present my papers requesting to leave my beloved Cuba. El Ministerio willingly terminated my position as administrator and director of the Ernest Hemingway Museum. As punishment for my uncooperativeness, they sent me to work two years of hard labor cutting sugar cane in the fields in the province of Camagüey, on the other side of the island, far away from my family. I lived in overcrowded camps filled with men like me who simply wanted to take our families and leave the country. The government was determined to humiliate us, to break our spirits—"apatria" (stateless) or "gusano" (worm) were the common terms for anyone who wished to leave Cuba. But most of us persevered, and in the end we got out.

Before leaving the Finca, I stopped and turned back and took it all in—the house, the gardens, the garage, the small ceiba tree. They should have never cut down the old tree. I'm glad I wasn't there when it happened.

That evening Raúl and I learned that the manuscript and photographs I had left behind with a friend had been lost. We were devastated. My blood pressure rose, and I had to take a heart pill. Always my caretaker, Raúl walked me to the bedroom and sat me on the bed. He tried to calm me down, encouraging me not to give up.

"We have other photographs. And you still have your memory," he said.

"Pero, estoy viejo y cansado," I said. I told him I was old and tired. I didn't want to disappoint him. I always told him to never give up. So how could I? He had been so wonderful these past five months, always at our sides, speaking to us on the telephone every day and visiting on the weekends. I knew it would break his heart if I gave up.

"We can start from scratch. It will be better than what you had," Raúl said, looking into my eyes. "Remember what Papa Hemingway always told you: 'A man can be destroyed but not defeated.'"

He knew just what to say. He remembers every word I say and knows when to use them on me. Raúl also knows my stories by heart. We would do it for the family, he said. We would do it for Rodolfo, and especially for his girls. He knew I would respond to this. Yes, the family—what is most important in a person's life.

That night I couldn't sleep. Years of my own writing, countless precious photographs, and a wealth of autographed books from Papa Hemingway had been lost forever. Why had I not claimed them sooner? I was a fool to put such trust in a friend. The only reason I didn't leave them with my family was because I feared that if the government found out about their existence, they would search my family's home and confiscate them. For that reason only I entrusted them to a friend, not family. And now all those stories and evidence of wonderful, cherished moments were lost.

Lying in bed I felt my heart pound with rage. I was not going to let life cheat me again. I still remembered everything—crystal-clear recollections from the first day I met Hemingway to the last time I saw him and throughout the dark days following his death. I remembered it all—and no one could ever take those memories from me.

Then I remembered Papa's advice on reading and writing: when he was reading and writing, he preferred to stop at an important point in the story. For reading, he had explained to me, it made him want to go back and pick up the book again with interest and enthusiasm. If he stopped writing at a point where it was good and he knew exactly what was going to happen, at a point of high interest, it made his next day's work start easier. And I remembered how he liked to write in the mornings because, he said, his mind was clear and fresh from a night's rest.

I was relieved recalling his advice and eased into sleep.

THE FINCA

The Finca Vigía should be properly introduced before I begin my stories. After all, for two decades it was an important character in Hemingway's life, and mine.

When I close my eyes, I clearly see the grounds, the house, the rooms—details no matter how insignificant. Five long concrete steps lead to the main entrance of the house. The majestic ceiba tree shades the front of the house and menaces the roof with its branches. That ceiba was Hemingway's favorite tree. He did not allow anybody to trim, prune, or damage the tree while he lived there. Back in the mid-1940s I often spoke with a couple of men of about seventy who had been born in and lived in the pueblo their entire lives, the children of former African slaves. They remembered that ceiba being there when they were children.

Southeast from the main house is the garage. Original to the Finca, it had been built to house horse carriages. While minor modifications were made to accommodate Hemingway's three cars—the red Chrysler with the white top, the yellow Plymouth convertible, and the Buick stationwagon—it retained the Spanish colonial design. North of the garage is the bungalow, which served as a guest house for long-term visitors.

The house has three sets of French doors that open onto the terrace, which wraps around the house, becoming wider at the front of the house, facing south. In the front, a pergola provides comfortable shade during the hot summer months, a nice place to read and enjoy the breeze. Under the pergola, a ceramic-tile cistern holds rainwater.

On Wednesdays, Hemingway and Mary had their hair washed with rainwater by Lily, the manicurist. Mary believed it was good for the hair. From the back of the house, looking north, I see the beautiful city of Havana, the top of El Capitolio Nacional, and, on the left, El Monumento José Marti.

I enter the living room from the main entrance. This high-ceilinged, spacious room is approximately 44 feet long by 16 feet wide and is painted white. The walls are covered with safari trophies and artwork. The large oil canvas on the east wall was painted by Roberto Domingo, a French artist of Spanish descent whose work was strictly on or about bullfighting. This particular painting was used on the cover of an edition of *Death in the Afternoon*. The head of an impala gazelle used to hang to the left of the painting, a trophy from Papa's 1934 African safari. The oryx to the right he shot that same year in Kenya.

From the living room I walk north to the dining room, also painted white. No doors divide the rooms. Instead, two large columns support an arched entrance between them. On each column hangs a deer head, both shot in Sun Valley. On the east side of the dining room are six large windows, which are usually open to allow a breeze to flow through the house. The large table and chairs were designed by Mary and built by Pancho, the Spanish carpenter, out of precious Cuban mahogany. Hemingway usually sat at the end of the table with his back to the large windows, with Mary opposite him. If there were guests, he sat at the north end of the table with his back to the large French doors at the end of the dining room, with Mary to his right and the guests in their usual favorite seats. Both of these seats allowed Papa to contemplate his favorite painting, *The Farm,* by Joán Miró, which hung on the west wall of the dining room. In 1957 the Museum of Modern Art in New York persuaded Hemingway to lend them the painting for an exhibit. The painting never returned to Cuba. In 1986, in her will, Mary donated it to the National Gallery of Art, Washington, D.C. At the Finca it was replaced by the head of a male kudu shot in Masai territory in Tanzania in 1934 and described in *The Green Hills of Africa*. The other trophy higher on the wall is a giraffe gazelle killed during the 1953 safari.

Back in the living room, I stand behind the sofa table and see Hemingway's favorite chair at the southwest side of the room, close to the set of windows on the south wall. In that armchair he would sit and read in the middle of the afternoon and fall asleep with Blackie, his faithful dog, at his feet. Only special friends or guests were invited to sit in that chair. Next to the armchair stands a small table with an ice bucket, two kinds of whiskey, a bottle of dry vermouth, a bottle of Gordon's Gin, and some bottles of mineral and tonic water. The phonograph Lee Samuels gave his good friend is at the southwest end of the living room. Hemingway's taste in music was very eclectic. He enjoyed listening to a variety of styles, mostly classical music and jazz. His record collection includes Bach, Stravinsky, Benny Goodman, Louis Armstrong, Segovia, and even Marlene Dietrich, his dear friend. Two gazelle heads adorn the south wall of the living room. The large living room has four bookcases, two under the gazelles and two at the end of the living room on the west and north walls. Next to the bookcases on the north wall hangs a large bullfight poster designed by Roberto Domingo.

The bookcase on the west wall, by the entrance to Hemingway's workroom, displays a replica of Sputnik given to him by Anastas Mikoyan in 1960. When the former Russian head of state visited the Finca, he brought books, magazines, wooden dolls, vodka, wine, and caviar. He and Papa toasted their good health, and Papa told Mikoyan that vodka was great to gargle with to avoid colds and relieve sore throats—except one should never spit it out afterward. Above the bookcases on the wall hangs a replica of a Goya painting of one of the royal infants, a gift from Ernest to Mary during one of their European trips. On the north wall hangs the head of a deer Mary shot in Idaho.

The living room floor is covered with a Philippine matting that Hemingway bought in China in the early 1940s during his honeymoon with his third wife, Martha Gellhorn. He had telephoned Otto Bruce, a friend from his Key West days who took care of the Finca Vigía at the time, for the exact measurements of the living room and Martha's bedroom. The custom-made, hand-woven matting arrived at the Finca a couple of months later, and Bruce and the entire staff wrestled to place the 35-by-15-foot rug. It had been rolled up tight during the long boat trip, so when one end was placed on the floor the other curled up. I was about thirteen then and remember putting all the furniture on one side of the living room to keep the matting in place as the gardeners and servants stood on the other end to keep it flat until we could place the pieces of furniture. Some years later the matting in Martha's room was damaged by a leaking roof following a hurricane and had to be discarded.

From the living room I walk into Hemingway's workroom, where he wrote. About 16 feet by 14 feet, the room is on the west side of the house. It is as he left it in 1960, waiting for his return. The full-sized bed on the south wall, on which he read and slept siesta, was usually covered with correspondence, magazines, and books. Papa read several books at a time, placing one book face down to mark his place before picking up the next one. He did the same with magazines—*Life, Look, Field & Stream,* and *The New Yorker*. A bottle of Vichy mineral water stands on the floor next to the bed. He drank the water straight from the bottle and at room temperature. On a small wooden night table by the large window on the south wall, a pair of Hemingway's reading glasses rests on top of an issue of *Sea Frontiers* magazine. On the other side of the bed another night table stands and next to it a large wicker basket with three metal legs. The round, deep basket was where I placed newly arrived books, magazines, and correspondence, which Papa would browse through at his convenience. A bookcase stands against the east wall, and a gazelle head from the 1934 safari hangs over it.

At one time a large oil painting hung on the south wall above the bed, *El Guitarrista* by Juan Grís. It was one of his favorite pieces, and he often spoke of what it meant to him. "René, I really love this painting," he said one day, contemplating the piece. "Now it's very valuable, but I love it for the nostalgia. It represents a special time in my life. If there is ever a fire in the house, try to save this one first." He hesitated. "On second thought, forget what I just said. No painting is worth risking a human life for." *El Guitarrista* reminded Papa of his Paris years. The painting is now in Patrick Hemingway's private collection. *The Jungle,* by Andre Masson, also once hung in his workroom.

Hemingway usually worked standing in front of the bookcase, which had been designed so that he could place his old Royal typewriter on top and work without having to lean over. But somehow the bookcase was not built to the correct height. When Papa discovered it was short by almost four inches, he simply placed a thick book on the top shelf and placed his typewriter on the book, saying, "We don't have to do anything else. It's fine this way."

He had great respect and love for his work, and tremendous discipline. By 6:00 A.M. he would be up and quietly walking through the house trying not to disturb anyone. He was proud of being able to walk very quietly. "It goes with being a hunter," he often said. My room was right under Mary's bedroom. Being a light sleeper, I always heard him get up no matter what. He was a large man, and the floors of the house were old and creaky. And though I didn't have to be up until 8:00 A.M. to serve breakfast, I often rose early, went upstairs, and watched him do his morning stretches and leg raises. Afterward he went to his workoom and started writing. During the hot summer months he wore shorts, no shirt, and was barefoot. If the floor was cold, he wore his old moccasins or stood on top of the kudu skin in front of the bookcase.

Every morning he sharpened several pencils and placed them next to his typewriter and then clipped several plain sheets of white paper onto the clipboard. Once I offered to sharpen his pencil for him, but he told me, "It's part of my work." When he finished a sheet, he unclipped it and put it face down on top of the bookcase and placed a large mineral rock on top as a paperweight. He wrote descriptions and narration on the typewriter; dialogue he handwrote in pencil. At the end of a workday, Papa counted the words and noted the number and date on the inside cover of the paper box. He then placed the manuscripts in the box and closed the lid so that no one could see his notes. The next day, pencil in hand, he read all he had written the day before. Sometimes I saw him cross words out or change them, but I never saw him discard anything. He wrote with confidence and precision.

Breakfast consisted of a glass of grapefruit or orange juice, a teapot with enough hot water for two servings of black tea (no sugar), two fried or hard-boiled eggs, two slices of toast, and three strips of bacon. One of the eggs and two strips of the bacon were served in a separate bowl for Boise, his favorite cat. Boise, or Boy, as Hemingway sometimes called him, usually shared Papa's siesta as well, often sleeping on Hemingway's chest. Once he asked if Boise slept with me when he was away. I told him that when he was away, Boise preferred to sleep all day and at night go out and hunt fruit rats.

I was the only person who entered his room while Hemingway worked. I tried not to disturb him. One morning, I didn't hear the click-clack of the typewriter and hurried into the room to collect the breakfast dishes, but there he was writing dialogues. I quickly backed out of the room. He called me back and asked if there was anything wrong, why I had left the room. I told him that there was nothing wrong, that I didn't want to disturb him. He smiled and said that I didn't disturb him at all. "Come in and do what you have to do and make-believe I'm not even here. You don't bother me, and I don't bother you." He told me how he felt better knowing I was around because he knew I would intercept anyone who really would disturb him. But even so, I tried not to enter his room unless he called me, or in case of an emergency. And I, too, tried to walk quietly like a hunter.

The impressive head of an African cape buffalo hangs on the east wall of his study, which is adjacent to his workroom on the north side and has the same dimensions as the workroom. Hemingway shot the African buffalo in Masai country and described the series of events surrounding the hunt in *The Short Happy Life of Francis Macomber.* Underneath stands another bookcase, on top of which is the small, powerful rifle used to kill the impressive beast. Pauline Pfeiffer, his second wife, also used that rifle during the 1934 safari. On top of an adjacent bookcase to the south there used to rest three small paintings: *Monument in Arbert* by Paul Klee, *El Torero* by Juan Grís, and another painting by Andre Masson. Mary Hemingway took them out of Cuba in 1961, after Papa's death. These two bookscases and a narrower one are filled with many precious volumes of classic literature.

In the middle of the study is a large wooden bureau that holds an eclectic array of souvenirs from around the world. Whenever Hemingway returned from a trip, he left small mementoes and empty gun cartridges on top of the writing desk. The large metal key lying on top of the bureau was a gift from the mayor of Matanzas when Papa returned from Europe on the transatlantic steamer *Ile de France.* Small hand-carved wooden figurines from the 1954 African safari are also scattered on the bureau. Hemingway's oldest son's, Jack's, military stripes are displayed underneath the glass that covers the top of the bureau, as well as a photograph of Mary in her World War II war correspondent uniform and another of Marlene Dietrich.

On the west wall of the room there is a shoe rack with several pairs of shoes, including his favorite old, beat-up moccasins. When I met him in the early 1940s, he wore sandals, but he stopped wearing them years later. The top shelf of the shoe rack is covered by a matador's cape given to him by Sidney Franklin, the famous American bullfighter and Hemingway's friend. On top of the cape are several exotic knives: a Japanese dagger, a large antique hunting knife, two bayonet knives from different wars, and two puntillas, which are used in bullfights to deliver the coup de grace to the bull. One of the most interesting items in the collection is an African knife covered with beautiful colorful beads and shells; it has a matching belt made out of antelope skin. Several walking sticks lean next to the shoe rack; these were given to Papa in 1953 by the Masai and Wakamba tribes.

Papa's bathroom is on the northwest side of the house, accessible from the study. Hemingway weighed himself every day on his bathroom scale after finishing his morning exercises. On the walls around the scale are dated weigh-in notes and comments. He started this morning ritual after returning from Africa in 1954, after he had been badly injured in two airplane crashes. He was never the same physically after the accidents and was under increased medical attention.

In his bathroom is a bookcase. Papa said to me once, "My profession is to write, and as a writer I must read all the time. I don't like to waste any time, and even in here I can take advantage of the opportunity and read." He would leave books open, face down, on top of the water tank or on the edge of the tub or on the floor. So Mary designed a bookcase and had Pancho build it. The first shelf holds books and the top shelf medicines, ointments, and toiletries. But it also has two interesting containers on it: a large glass jar with a chameleon preserved in alcohol and a bottle of Haig Pinch Scotch Whiskey. The chameleon had bravely confronted one of the large fighting cats, Big Goats, or Bigotes, as we sometimes called him, and Hemingway preserved it in the glass jar to display its unquestionable courage, will to fight, and nobility. And on his last African safari, he learned that the Masai tribe used lion lard as an ointment for muscle aches. After a successful lion hunt, he brought some of the lard home to Cuba in the only container available, an empty bottle of Haig Pinch.

The library is on the north side of the house. It measures about 26 feet long by 16 wide and has floor-to-ceiling bookcases on the east and west walls of the room. Next to one of the bookcases on the east side is a three-step ladder with wheels used to reach the top shelves. At one time there were more than 8,500 books in the house, with no order to their placement. There were books on the floor, tables, shelves, and in baskets all over the house. Not in alphabetical order, the books were simply grouped by subject matter or author.

On the floor of the library, a camel saddle Papa brought back from Cairo in 1954 is used as a foot stool. The room has two large windows on the north wall. Between the windows, a pair of French doors provides access to the terrace. On the south wall hangs an unfired ceramic plate of a bull's head Pablo Picasso made for Hemingway during a trip to Europe in 1957. On top of one of the bookcases on the east wall are two glass vases: one a nineteenth-century pink Grandbury and the other from Venice. Next to the vases is a hand-carved figurine of a squatting man, which, according to African belief, was supposed to protect and guard plantations and properties and their owners from evil spirits.

On the west wall hung the skin and head of a black-maned lion Mary shot during the 1954 safari. She took her lion back to the States in 1961, where I saw it the times I visited her apartment in New York City. Mary enjoyed taking her siesta on the long couch in the library, from which she admired her lion trophy. The couch, covered with the skin and head of a leopard, was also Gary Cooper's favorite place to sleep in the house, since its length accomodated his frame, which was too long for the guest beds. Behind the couch stands a long, semi-circular majagua wood table with leg reliefs shaped like mango leaves. This is another of Mary's designs.

Hemingway wrote his letters at the desk in the library. He used the bill of a swordfish as a paperweight for outgoing correspondence. Also on the desk was his personal stamp, which read "I never write letters," which he used to "answer" unwanted correspondence. It was in this room, at this desk, where he made the final edits on his work. After reviewing the final draft, he made the necessary corrections in pencil.

East of the library is the guest room. It used to be the cats' room, but in 1949 the cats were moved out of the house and into the new tower. The room was then prepared for visitors. Painted a light pink, the guest room, or the Venetian Room, is as big as the library. Simply decorated, it has two beds with a night table in between, two majagua armchairs, two bookcases filled with books, and a dressing table. On the dressing table is a 12-inch-thick white candle that was given to Hemingway on his fiftieth birthday by Lee Samuels. It was useful during the blackouts caused by bad weather. On the east wall behind the beds hangs a watercolor given to Hemingway by a French artist who lived in Havana and often asked me for permission to draw and paint on the Finca's grounds.

At the end of the guest room, on the west wall, is a Chinese tempera, a gift from Winston Guest when Hemingway bought the house in 1939. The other painting on the east side of the room is a portrait of Hemingway painted by my younger brother Oscar. My family lived next to the entrance of the Finca Vigía, and Hemingway often stopped by our home to chat with my parents. He always admired Oscar's paintings and one day bought a set of oil paints and brushes for him. As a token of appreciation, Oscar painted his portrait. Hemingway, very pleased with it, had it framed and hung it in the Venetian Room.

Mary's room is located on the east side of the house. Here, I stand in the doorway and look north outside the two small windows and see the kitchen and stairs. The king-sized bed in the room was designed by Otto Bruce after Hemingway married Martha Gellhorn. Mary made a lot of changes when she moved into the Finca, and that room was no exception. She had a bookcase made to go on the headrest of the bed, and there she kept her gardening, cooking, and home decorating books. The rest of the furniture was designed by her and made by Pancho. Another bookcase at the foot of the bed has more of her favorite books, and on the top of the bookcase are her favorite magazines. The bureau and chest of drawers were made from Cuban mahogany and feature beautiful, detailed ornamental designs. The chair made from the same wood is upholstered in the skin of a shark Mary caught during a fishing trip to Cayo Paraíso. An antique Venetian mirror hangs on the north wall, and to the left of the mirror once hung a fourteenth-century Madonna icon of 23-karat gold leaf that was purchased during one of Hemingway's trips to Italy. A portrait of a young Ernest by Waldo Pierce, with the dedication "For Ernest alias Kid Balzac," also hung on that wall. Above one of the bookcases on the east wall hangs an antelope head, one of Mary's trophies from the 1953 Kenya safari. The room's bathroom holds mostly Mary's toiletries.

In Mary's room they slept and made plans for their trips and decided how they wanted to live their lives. Papa slept on the right side of the bed facing south to the windows, which provided a great view of the ceiba.

The tower, completed in 1949, was built close to the main house. It has four levels, including the basement, which was once used as a carpenter's shop. The second level is the cats' room, with a sloped floor that could be hosed off and three shelves for napping felines. The third level is used as storage for skis, hunting boots, fishing rods and reels, African lances, rifles, and numerous animal trophies, including a stuffed black bear. The fourth level is the studio made specifically for Hemingway. A spacious and airy room with large windows on all sides and a beautiful panoramic view of Havana and the sea, the studio is furnished with bookcases, a large writing table, and a leather chair. From here there is access to a spiral staircase that leads to the roof.

It didn't matter where Papa Hemingway traveled; he was always happy to return to the Finca Vigía—his Cuban paradise—where he lived the longest and felt at ease with the land and its people, where he relaxed and entertained visitors from all over the world.

The Finca became my paradise, too. It was a place so different and unique from anything I had ever known or would ever come to know.

CALL HIM PAPA

I was born on August 30, 1929, in El Vedado, a beautiful suburb of Havana. My parents named me René Luis Rosa de La Caridad Villarreal Vergara and my identical twin brother Luis René Rosa de La Caridad Villarreal Vergara. We were born on the day of Santa Rosa de Lima. My parents were devout Catholics and followed the tradition of including our saint's name among our middle names. Unknown to them, the records department in El Vedado made a mistake and listed us as girls: Luisa Renee Rosa de La Caridad and Renee Luisa Rosa de La Caridad. (We were in our late teens before we discovered the error when Luis tried to acquire a driver's license for a job at the waterworks company.) Blessed with healthy twin boys, my parents dedicated us to the blessed mother, La Virgen del Cobre, Cuba's patron saint.

I grew up in San Francisco de Paula, a town about ten miles southeast of downtown Havana. The small pueblo was founded by Franciscan monks, one of the first monastic orders to arrive in Cuba around 1570. Five wealthy families owned most of the land: the Glins, the Panteons, Don Pepe, the Belicas, and Don Julian Rodríguez. Don Julian Rodríguez owned the vaquería, a parcel of land southeast of Finca Vigía. Most of the people in the pueblo knew each other. It was a poor town with simple customs and even simpler laws.

My childhood home was near the entrance to the Finca Vigía. Our modest house was always filled with laughter and the joy of children. We were a large family of eight—my father, Mario, and mother, Felita, and us six children: Heliodoro, Luis, me, Oscar, Rodolfo (whom we all called Popito), and our baby sister, Nilda. My brothers and I adored Nilda and watched over her as if she were a daughter, not a sister.

Both of my parents worked very hard to provide food and clothing for the family. My father, who was fondly called Coco even by my mother, worked as a cook at a hospital in Havana. My mother took in laundry. They were honest, humble people who raised their children to be the same way. It was not easy feeding and clothing the six of us in those days, but they managed. We went to school clothed and with shoes—more than some children from the pueblo even hoped for.

I remember clearly the very first time I saw Ernest Hemingway. It was in 1939. I was almost 10 years old. I was playing baseball in the street in front of the Finca Vigía with Heliodoro, Luis, and other boys from the pueblo—Pepitico, El Calluco, El Gallego, and Pituche. We had stopped midplay when we saw a vulture trying to find refuge by the side fence of the Finca. We surrounded the bird, not allowing it to escape. Just then a large dark sedan drove up and stopped by the front gates of the Finca. Two men stepped out of the car.

"Muchachos! What are you doing with that bird?" asked one of the men in Spanish. We told him that we were just playing with the vulture. He then told us to leave the injured bird alone. We did as the man requested and the vulture disappeared behind the fence of the Finca Vigía. The men walked back to the car at the front gate of the Finca.

In those days, cars didn't pass through the pueblo very often. Only well-to-do people, government officials, or diplomats could afford automobiles. The man who had spoken to us was tall and strong, with long hair and a thick mustache. He wore a short-sleeve shirt, shorts, and leather sandals. The other man was dressed the same but was not as tall. They tried to open the gate and after a couple of tries called us over.

"Is this the house of Mr. Roger Joseph D'orn?" the tall man with the mustache asked. From his accented Spanish we realized he was a foreigner, most likely americano. A couple of the boys confirmed that it was. El americano asked if we knew how to open the gate. Some of the boys knew the trick to the gates and forced the lock in no time. (The chain and lock were only placed around the handles of the gate, giving the apperance it was locked.) El americano smiled, put his hand in his pocket, and handed each of us a dollar. We thanked him repeatedly jumping around and clapping. Clearly embarrassed, el americano blushed and tried to calm our enthusiasm, tried to settle us down. Perhaps he didn't realize that this was extraordinary for us sons of strong, hardworking men who didn't earn a dollar for a good day's labor.

El americano asked what we had been doing before their arrival. We told him we'd been playing baseball. He squatted down to speak with us at eye level and asked us with what equipment. We explained that we made the ball ourselves from strips of old rags and reinforced it with string to make it harder. The bat is just the handle of an old broom, we told him, and we played a manos limpia, without gloves, and home and first bases were flat pieces of wood and cardboard. I imagine that the circumstances, ingenuity, and simplicity of our baseball team aroused his curiosity. We also told him that we couldn't play inside the Finca Vigía because el señor D'orn would let the dogs loose or, even worse, have Don Pedro, the gardener, chase us out. El señor D'orn didn't want any of the children from the pueblo on his property playing or picking fruit. He would let the fruit fall and spoil on the ground before offering it to any child from San Francisco de Paula.

El americano stood up, stretched his long legs, and turned to his friend, who had remained silent all this time, and joked with him in English. They both laughed. Then he said to us that he was going to speak to that very nice man who lived there—smiling and pointing to the gates—and, if the price was right, he may live there himself. He said that if that happened, he would make sure we will be allowed to go and pick whatever fruit we like and play baseball in the open field. He also said that he had three sons, "and two of them are about your age," and soon they were coming to visit him. He said he would like it if they had friends to play with.

"We can put home base over there, first base there, second there, and third over on this side," he said, pointing to several places on the large open field. "I will get equipment—baseballs, gloves, and bases." We clapped and jumped up and down with enthusiasm again. I remember how he blushed and tried to settle us down again. The two men said good-bye to us and got in their car and drove through the large, white wooden gate and up the narrow, inclined road to the house.

I don't remember exactly how much time passed between that first time I saw Hemingway and when he was actually living at the Finca Vigía, but I do remember that he kept his promise and let us children enter the property and pick from the array of wonderful fruit. In turn, we only had to promise not to throw rocks or damage any of the trees.

I learned several years later how Hemingway came to buy the Finca Vigía. In 1939, back from the Spanish Civil War, he was staying in suite 511, his favorite room, in the Hotel Ambos Mundos, the hotel located in the city of Havana between Obispo and Monserrat streets. It was owned by his good friend Manuel Asped, who later became a good friend of mine. Hemingway liked the quiet and tranquility of the hotel. It was there where he started to write *For Whom the Bell Tolls.* After a day's work in the hotel, Hemingway often walked to his favorite bar, El Floridita. When Martha Gellhorn joined him in Cuba in 1939, she thought the room was too small and dirty for her to share and found a rental ad in the newspaper and pursuaded Hemingway to see the property. Though his initial reaction to the condition of the house was not favorable, in 1939 he rented the Finca Vigía for 100 Cuban pesos a month from Roger Joseph D'orn Duchamp and then purchased it in December of 1940 for 18,500 Cuban pesos. The Finca was the first house he owned that had not been given to him.

Built by Catalan architect Miguel Pascula Baguer in 1886, the Finca Vigía was used by the Spanish army as a lookout fort to observe Havana—hence the name Vigía, from vigilar, "to keep vigil" or "look out for." After the Spanish-American War, the Spanish army abandoned the house and set fire to the property. Fortunately, the wooden structure was not completely destroyed. It was restored by one of its subsequent owners.

Just as he had told us boys, Hemingway's three sons arrived the summer of 1940 to spend their vacation at the Finca: John (Jack), whom everyone called Bumby; Patrick, nicknamed Mouse; and the youngest, Gregory, whom we all called Gigi. My brothers and I met Hemingway's sons on the field where we played baseball. Bumby, Mouse, and Gigi spoke Spanish well and we all got along fine. Bumby, who was around seventeen years old, was five years or more older than most of the group, and preferred to be by himself. He was more interested in the activities of a young adolescent than those of little boys. Hemingway and Gigi took a special liking to my youngest brother and asked Popito and his friend Fico to run errands for the Finca and help tend to the two cats and two dogs. They each received a small wage for their work. Gigi, Fico, and Popito, all of them around eight or nine years old, became inseparable. Popito and Fico felt right at home at the Finca Vigía, going in and out of the house whenever they pleased.

Hemingway did indeed buy us baseball equipment and uniforms and even organized a team he called Las Estrellas de Gigi, in honor of his youngest son. My brothers and I, along with several of our friends from the pueblo, made up the teams. We played against each other on the Finca grounds, and sometimes Hemingway took us along with him to the shooting and hunting club, El Club de Cazadores del Cerro, in Havana. At El Cerro we were allowed to order soft drinks. But soon that became a problem, because most of the players asked for one soda pop after another and more time was spent going to the bathroom than playing baseball. From then on Hemingway told us that whoever hit a home run or a three-base hit would get a Coca-Cola as a prize.

We played our games on an open field opposite the shooting range, out of harm's way. At first we played against each other, but eventually the other members of the club brought their sons along to play against us. The adults practiced their shooting, drank, and talked while the children played baseball. The members did not mind us playing at the private club because they got the opportunity to spend a sporting afternoon with Ernest Hemingway. At the time, we boys knew that he was americano, rich, and nice to us, but we didn't know the extent of his fame or what he did.

It was difficult for us boys to pronounce "Hemingway," so we started to call him "Papa," as his sons did. Hemingway didn't mind having a dozen children screaming "Papa! Papa!" and his friends, including Winston Guest, were amused and started to call him Papa as well.

Hemingway reciprocated by letting us know that Guest could also be called Wolfie. At six-five, Wolfie was big, strong, and athletic. Hemingway had met him in East Africa during the 1933 safari. He was one of Hemingway's closest friends in Cuba and also one of his favorite drinking partners. Together they created el definitivo, a blend of vodka, gin, tequila, rum, whiskey, tomato juice, and a lot of lime juice. The trick drink was intended to obliterate the Herrera brothers, the jai alai players, and Don Andrés, but most of the time Hemingway and Guest succumbed to their own concoction as well.

Hemingway and his friends joined our baseball games at the Finca and the club. They took turns at bat, and one of the younger boys from the team would run the bases for them. My brother Oscar ran the bases for Papa, whose hit usually resulted in a good enough run for Oscar to earn a Coca-Cola. On a particular day, we played a close game against some of the children of the patrons. Hemingway made a good hit and Oscar ran all the way to third base. Seizing the opportunity to make it all the way home, he kept running. The catcher from the other team protected home base. The throw from the outfielder came in and Oscar dove to home base. The catcher, an older and a much bigger boy, pushed Oscar out of the way. Oscar broke his left arm. Hemingway and Juan rushed Oscar to the Calixto Garcia Hospital in Havana.

Later that day, by the time Hemingway and Oscar arrived at my house, the rest of the team was waiting for them. Hemingway was very embarrassed and walked in holding Oscar by the hand. My brother's left arm was in a cast and sling. Papa apologized to my mother, who told him not to worry, because if it had not happened with him, it would have happened with someone else. "It's part of growing up," my mother said with no anger in her voice. Hemingway thanked her for being so understanding.

My parents were very happy that el americano allowed the children of the pueblo to play on his property, enjoy the cool waters of the pool, and pick the fruits growing at the Finca. There was a big difference between Mr. Way, as most of the adults in the pueblo called him, and the previous owner, Señor D'orn.

That first summer passed quickly for us. Before September, Bumby, Mouse, and Gigi headed back to the States to continue their studies. We were all sad to see them leave. "Even though my sons are not here, you can still use the baseball equipment and the boxing gloves," Hemingway said in a somber tone the same day his sons left. "All I ask is after you're done with them you put them back in the same place."

THE GARDENER

When Hemingway bought the Finca Vigía in 1940, he told Señor D'orn that he would honor the servants' positions and keep their service. The majordomo at that time was a Jamaican named Luis. Also on staff were the cook, a short, heavyset Spanish woman named María, and the head gardener, Don Pedro. Not only the head gardener, Don Pedro was the head of the servants. He had been working at the Finca the longest. A Spaniard from Cataluña, Don Pedro was a short, stocky man with a reddish complexion, a full head of white hair, and a long white mustache. He was the same gardener who used to chase us trespassing children off the Finca's grounds by wielding a machete over his head and running after us screaming obscenities like a crazy man. We were young and fast. He never got close to catching us. But he did scare the living daylights out of us.

Don Pedro's torment began when Hemingway prohibited the pruning of the gardens and trees and told him he could no longer chase us out of the Finca. Now he only was to keep the garden and trees healthy from damaging insects and irrigate the grounds. Don Pedro had always prided himself on the beautiful grounds of the estate. But now we children were Ernest Hemingway's guests, and we were allowed on the property and permitted to pick fruit. I can only imagine the frustration poor Don Pedro must have felt seeing the same kids he took so much pleasure chasing off the property now parading in front of him, smiles on our dirty little faces as we filled our bellies with fruit and played as if we were in our own home.

I remember the day when a small group of us boys explored the Finca grounds with Papa. We came across a large wooden birdcage that must have been left there by Señor D'orn. Hemingway examined the poor condition of the birds—little water and no food. It was obvious that the cage had not been maintained in days. He found a metal rod and forced open the lock, setting the birds free. "I don't want caged birds on my property," he said, visibly angry, "and even less so in this condition." He looked at each of us sternly and admonished, "Don't ever hurt any of the animals here. They should be allowed to enjoy the surroundings and live as free as we do."

Later that afternoon, Don Pedro made his rounds and came across the open, empty birdcage. He looked at us playing nearby and took the machete out of its sheath and, like the devil, ran toward us yelling, "I'm going to cut your ugly little heads off! Bastards! Filthy bastards!"

He had chased us before, and we always outran him with ease, but this time the ferocity of his anger paralyzed us. Instead of running to the gate of the Finca as we usually did, we ran to the house. Hemingway sat reading under the pergola on the terrace. We reached him screaming and crying, "Don Pedro, Don Pedro. He's after us!" Tears ran down our cheeks, and we trembled in fear.

Don Pedro arrived at the terrace a few seconds later, gasping for air and red in the face. He was gnashing his teeth. His eyes bulged out. The machete was still in his hand. "Filthy bastards! They destroyed the birdcage and freed all the birds!" he screamed enraged, trying to suck in air.

"Hand over your machete!" Hemingway held out his hand demanding the machete. He told the gardener that he had freed the birds and that on his property he did not wish to have birds in a cage, never mind in such miserable conditions. "Don't ever threaten these children again. They are my guests in this house!" He waited for Don Pedro to relinquish the machete.

The gardener handed over the machete and, shrugging his shoulders, asked Hemingway what his responsibilities were at the Finca, since he couldn't prune or trim the trees and garden or run the children off the property anymore. Not waiting for an answer, Don Pedro walked down the stairs, turning back to give us boys an evil look. We clung to Hemingway, trembling, until he convinced us it was safe to go back and continue playing.

A few days later Hemingway made Don Pedro destroy the birdcage and had him build a tool shed in its place. After completing the shed, Don Pedro submitted his resignation and left the Finca. Two days later his wife, Margarita—la Catalana, as as she was known in the pueblo—came to the Finca looking for her husband. She hadn't seen him in two days and wondered if we knew of his whereabouts. We told her we had not seen Don Pedro since he left two days earlier, and Hemingway told Margarita that her husband had resigned and left with his last paycheck in hand. The poor woman searched for her husband all over San Francisco de Paula and neighboring towns.

A couple of days later, we were playing baseball at the Finca. We couldn't help but notice the foul stench coming from a well near where we played ball. The square solid-iron top of the well was pushed to one side. Sensing something was wrong, we slowly approached the dark hole and looked in. To our horror, we saw Don Pedro's body at the bottom of the well, his lifeless, bloated body floating face up in the water. Hundreds of green flies buzzed around it. Even more horrible was the sight of a young red and black chick pecking at the droning flies and rotting flesh. In sheer terror we ran screaming all the way to the gate of the Finca. The police were immediately notified, as was Don Pedro's wife, Margarita. After a formal investigation, the gardener's death was ruled a suicide. There had been no foul play, according to authorities. Hemingway offered to pay for the funeral arrangements. A couple of days later he ordered the well sealed with concrete in order to avoid any similar incidents or accidents.

In the pueblo no one wanted to acknowledge ownership of the chick that had been at the bottom of the well pecking at Don Pedro's body. It was common practice in each family to secretly mark the chickens in case any crossed backyards or were stolen. In my house we trimmed the tip of the right toe of the right leg of the chicks. Other families marked their chickens differently so there wouldn't be any confusion among the freely wandering birds. A chick with no mark would have had more than twenty people claiming ownership in the neighborhood. But not the chick from the water well. No one wanted it. It turned out lucky for the bird, because it never became soup or part of a dinner. The homeless chick lived on scraps around the Finca grounds and neighboring houses and grew to become a large, fine rooster. It died of old age.

For a long time we children had nightmares of Don Pedro drowning in the well. It took some time before we forgot the drowing and the bad dreams subsided and we were back playing at the Finca. But even then, once in a while we would catch ourselves looking over our shoulders toward the well. Death had visited to never quite leave again.

POPITO

Sometime after Don Pedro's death, three of my brothers, Fico, and I were in the middle of a ballgame with other boys from the pueblo (Oscar had stayed home drawing under the kitchen table, as he liked to do) when we heard the oxen-pulled wagon of the old guajiro, a man nicknamed Seboruco, "large rock," an old peasant not regarded as being very bright. We dropped the baseball equipment on the field and ran toward the guajiro and his wagon, catching up with him at the rear of the Finca's property and asking for a ride to the front entrance. After grunting a couple of times, he agreed. There were five of us, and we all didn't fit onto the back of the wagon, so Fico and Popito, the youngest, sat on the wooden crossbar that separated the oxen.

The dirt road was very uneven, with large rocks and ditches, making for a very bumpy ride. The wagon rocked back and forth, but we held on tight. Then one of the wheels went into a deep ditch and over a large rock and the wagon rocked severely. Popito, on the crossbar, lost his grip and fell to the ground. Before anyone knew what had happened, one of the wagon wheels rolled over him. The guajiro stopped the wagon. We jumped off to help Popito up. He bent over holding his stomach with both hands, crying, "It hurts! It hurts!"

The old guajiro nervously defended himself, saying we were the ones who asked for the ride and it was not his fault. He repeated this several times, shaking his head and talking to himself. Popito stayed bent over, holding his stomach and crying. There was grave pain on his face. We tried to carry him home, but he refused. He wanted to walk home without any help. We followed closely, not knowing what to do.

My mother was already waiting for us by the porch. She had heard the commotion and come out to see what was happening. She saw Popito's pain-stricken face and rushed to him. She carried him back to the porch holding him tight in her arms. She listened to the guajiro's version of the story and the same account from several of the boys. Crying in horror, she sent one of my brothers to the Finca to tell el americano that Popito had been in a serious accident.

In a few minutes, Juan arrived with the stationwagon. My mother carried Popito into the backseat and they went to the nearest first aid station at the Loma de los Zapotes a couple miles from our house. There the doctors rerouted them to Calixto Garcia Hospital in Havana. The injuries were too severe to be attended to at the small clinic. At Calixto Garcia, the doctors rushed Popito into surgery. But he died during the operation. The doctors said he had several ruptured vital organs and his chances for survival had been minimal.

It is sad to make funeral arrangements for anyone, but even more sad if the funeral arrangements are for an eight-year-old child. Hemingway asked my parents' permission to pay the funeral expenses. He also sent two flower arrangements—one on behalf of the Finca Vigía and the other from the employees. Hemingway's name did not appear on either one. I came to learn that he always preferred it to be done that way.

Several weeks passed. My family was in luto, mourning the death of our Popito. At that time it was customary in Cuba to mourn the death of a loved one for six months or even a year. We missed our little brother dearly and faced the fact that we would never play with him again. The days passed with us sitting in the living room, my mother crying in her bedroom, and my father at work. The only door that was open in the house was the back door, to allow a breeze to flow through the house.

One afternoon not long after Popito's accident, we heard someone come in through the back door. Papa Hemingway walked into the living room and greeted us. He then asked to speak to either one of our parents. My mother came out of the bedroom wiping tears from her eyes.

"Señora, pardon the intrusion, but I want to let you know that el secretario's accident was not my fault," Hemingway said, looking into my mother's eyes. Gigi and Papa had fondly nicknaned Popito "the secretary" when he started to run errands at the Finca. My mother told Papa that she was aware we were the ones who had abandoned the baseball game to ride the wagon. He then asked her why the children were not allowed to play in the Finca anymore. "We're all sad at the Finca. We loved el secretario and miss him," he said with his head down. "The other boys don't come to play either. The Finca is empty without them. Señora, I want to have one of your sons always helping around the household." Hemingway looked at us.

My mother agreed to let one of us go. She said that she couldn't spare Heliodoro because he had too many chores. But that wasn't really the case. My mother knew how mischievous Heliodoro was and did not want to have Hemingway return in a couple of days with some sort of complaint. Papa said that Oscar reminded him too much of el secretario and would rather not ask him. He then asked if one of the twins could go with him. Luis didn't want to go, so Papa asked me if I wanted to help around the Finca after school. I agreed. "Can he go up to the Finca with me now?" Hemingway asked my mother. He thanked her and we left the house.

As we walked through the gate, Papa Hemingway put his hand on my shoulder. "I want you to feel at home. Come every day after school, help me tend the dogs and cats, and run some errands for María. Think of the Finca as your own home. You can come and leave as you please."

As we walked up to the house, past the baseball field, I couldn't help but look in the direction of the water well.

WORKING IN PARADISE

La Finca was paradise to an eleven-year-old boy. The rooms were filled with heads of antelope, gazelle, and other animals I had seen only in schoolbooks. The spacious rooms were covered with interesting, colorful art and images of bullfighters. As I swept the terrace in the afternoons, I was mesmerized by the exotic music played on the phonograph. The vegetation surrounding the house was luscious, with many different kinds of fruits, and it was in the cool waters of the Finca's pool where I learned how to swim.

In my first few days at the Finca, Hemingway instructed me on how to tend to the two dogs and the two cats that were the only pets at that time. Uncle Buffie and Princessa, both Persians, lived inside the house. I met Gang and Lane, the two short-haired white and brown German pointers, by their doghouse. We became friends immediately. He also took me to the post office in the pueblo and introduced me to Señor Mancebo, the postmaster and, according to Hemingway, a very efficient telegraph operator. And I also met Valentin Mesa, the butcher, who supplied the meat for the household and for the cats and dogs.

I learned that Wednesday was the day Hemingway's friends came for lunch and stayed on for dinner. The usual guest list included Don Andrés Untzain, a Basque priest Papa met during the Spanish Civil War. Don Andrés was punished for sympathizing with the wrong side during the war and was sent to Cuba to preach in a small church about thirty miles east of the Finca, attended mostly by poverty-stricken blacks. Among the other guests were a Spaniard named Roberto Herrera Sotolongo and his brother, José Luis; a republican doctor Hemingway also met during the Spanish Civil War, Don Juan Duñabeitia (who was called Siskie or Simbad); Elicio Argüelles, a well-to-do Cuban who sometimes fished with Papa and practiced shooting at El Club de Cazadores; Mario Menocal Jr., who everyone called Mayito, the wealthy son of Cuba's third president. Dr. Cucu Kholy and his American wife, Joy, also came to dinner, but usually only when Martha was present.

Hemingway did not socialize much with his wealthy businessman neighbor Frank Steinhart Jr., who owned a great property east of the Finca and whose father once owned the Havana Electrical Car Company. Ever since I can remember, Papa and Steinhart did not get along and behaved as if they were feuding warlords. I don't know if it was because of Hemingway's dislike of Steinhart's pretentious airs or because Papa had simply strained his neighbor's patience by hurling firecrackers over the property line and engaging in other sorts of irritating practical jokes.

Fico returned to the Finca and worked with me. It didn't take long to realize that he was lazy and didn't like doing his chores. He was also mischievous and devilish and disliked animals to the point of being abusive toward them. Whenever he walked close to one of the cats or dogs, he hit them for no reason, other than for the pure joy it gave him. The animals avoided him. He was two years younger than me but had the malice of an ancient demon.

One day while we were feeding Gang and Lane, Fico kicked Gang on the left shoulder. The poor dog let out a painful shriek and ran. I grabbed Fico by the neck and told him that if he ever did that again, it would be the last thing he would do with a full set of teeth in his mouth. The next morning, Papa Hemingway discovered a lump on Gang's left shoulder and called the veterinarian, Dr. Lagarde, who told Papa that the dog must have been hit very hard to cause such a swelling. He eventually found out it had been Fico. It was quite obvious that the dogs came to me whenever I called, yet they wanted nothing to do with Fico, no matter how hard he tried beckoning them. Hemingway told Fico not to come back to work at the Finca. Fico's father came the next day pleading on his son's behalf, Papa gave in and allowed the boy to return with the condition that Fico was to have no more contact with the cats and dogs.

María, the cook, was always sweet to us boys. In the late afternoon she served the staff dinner in the pantry. She called for Fico and me from the kitchen steps. Fico always dropped whatever he was doing and trampled whatever or whomever on his way to get to dinner. But I used to hide, or I politely refused dinner. Certainly I was hungry, and the meal always smelled delicious, but I couldn't bring myself to eat such good food when my brothers and sister back home were eating rice and beans with no meat. The times María managed to sit me at the table, I stared at the food, my eyes welling with tears. "Eat, eat! Look at yourself! You're nothing but skin and bones," she would yell, very frustrated, and then threaten to hit me on the head with the meat mallet. I knew her threats weren't real.

During one of those episodes, Hemingway heard the commotion from the living room and came to the pantry to find me sitting at the table crying and María holding the meat mallet in her hand. When she suddenly stopped her rant, I looked up and saw Papa shushing her with his index finger over his lips. He asked her what the problem was.

She explained my refusal to eat. "Señor, he's a good boy. Works very hard. Everywhere you send him he goes running. Doesn't misbehave. And he is respectful. But he doesn't want to eat come dinner time. He cries, runs away, and hides."

Hemingway asked me if I was hungry or didn't like the food. I didn't answer. I didn't want him to know the reason why I wouldn't eat María's meals. He told María not to force me to eat. She said she was at her wits' end not knowing the reason I wouldn't have dinner. Hemingway asked me again, but I wouldn't answer him. Crying, I ran out of the kitchen and hid.

María was a smart, persistent woman, and one day she finally broke down my defenses and got an answer out of me. She then told Hemingway the reason why I refused the meals. He told her to make extra food and give it to me to take home. That evening I went home with a cantina from María. My mother asked why I was bringing food home and became very upset, thinking I had asked for it or, even worse, stolen it. I told her that I knew not to steal or beg and also to respect my elders. I told her that María said el americano asked her to do it. My mother didn't respond. That evening my brothers and little sister were happy—we ate well and I felt good sharing the food with them. It was delicious. María was a great cook, and the following morning I complimented her on it.

A couple of months later, with a letter of recommendation from Hemingway, my father got a better-paying job at another hospital and was allowed to bring home the leftover food from the kitchen. Once the financial situation in my house improved, I didn't hesitate to eat whatever was offered to me at the Finca.

Papa Hemingway became interested in the cockfights in the early 1940s, even allowing Pichilo, the gardener, to breed and train cocks at the Finca. Hemingway's friend Paco Garay, a Spaniard with many contacts in diverse political circles, worked in customs and immigrations at the Havana airport. Garay had alerted Papa, Pichilo, and me of a confiscated shipment of Spanish roosters. Those roosters were bred with our criollos, and we started a great stock of fighting cocks.

Once we had a good fighter, Papa, Pichilo, Juan, and I visited the fighting arenas in the neighboring towns. One of the arenas was called Habana Guanabacoa, located in Guanabacoa; the one we usually frequented was La Valla de Otilio in El Cotorro. When we arrived at the arena, Papa usually purchased three cases of beer—one Hatuey, one Polar, and one Cristal. He also bought two bottles of rum. He instructed the owner of the arena to offer a free beer or shot of rum to the attending guajiros. For himself, he carried in the front pocket of his pants a shiny metal flask filled with either vodka or whiskey.

Pichilo was in charge of presenting and fighting the cocks. Juan stayed outside with the car. He didn't care much for the fights. At La Valla de Otilio, the big gamblers sat ringside. Hemingway, however, liked to sit on the top bleachers away from the mayhem of the betting. I sat with him, among old friends from the pueblo. The times Gary Cooper visited Cuba, he joined us at the cockfights. The three of us sat happily on the bleachers. Both felt more comfortable with the simple, common folk instead of the rich and professional gamblers. Sometimes they even drank from the rum bottle that was being passed around.

Hemingway met Gary Cooper at the Sun Valley Lodge in Idaho in the fall of 1940. Cooper had starred in the film versions of *A Farewell to Arms* and *For Whom the Bell Tolls.* The two became great friends, respecting and admiring each other throughout their lives. Cooper was my favorite guest to visit the Finca Vigía. He was a generous, courteous, and unpretentious man. You would never think that he was a famous Hollywood movie star. Unexpected and unannounced, he would arrive at the Finca and stay for a few days—to get away from the mayhem and craziness of a film set or simply to visit his friend. He drove himself in and out of the Finca and waved at the star-struck onlookers from the pueblo. After his stays at the Finca, he left envelopes for the staff and had me or Papa distribute the gifts. But always after he'd left.

THE GHOST IN THE DARKNESS

When I started working at the Finca, Martha Gellhorn was the lady of the house. A sophisticated, attractive, independent woman, she didn't approve much of having the local kids running freely around the Finca and swimming in the pool. I had little contact with her. I only heard the arguments between her and Papa. It wasn't long before she started spending more time away on *Collier's* assignments than at the Finca. I don't know what Martha Gellhorn and Hemingway argued about, but I do recall the arguments were extremely heated, loud, and frequent.

When Martha was away, Hemingway entertained himself in the afternoons by joining us kids in baseball games or by teaching us how to box with boxing gloves he had purchased along with the baseball equipment. As I excelled at my after-school responsibilities at the Finca, Hemingway's trust in me grew. When he realized my frustrations on the baseball field—that I couldn't hit or catch the ball well—he took the extra time to teach me how to box. When I didn't have school, he gave me lessons in the morning after I fed the cats. He had me use his stomach as a punching bag. I was strong and agile and learned a great number of boxing combinations. I also had a good defense. I developed the reputation as being a good, tough boxer, and boys from the pueblo and other neighboring towns came to challenge me. Almost every week I had a new challenger come to the Finca to defeat me, Kid Vigía. Hemingway was clearly very pleased that I, his student, was such a good boxer. And I was proud to make him happy. I loved the sport. I loved seeing the fear in my opponent's eyes. I loved winning. I was a good fighter—strong, fast, fearless.

But Papa Hemingway taught me so much more than just how to box, shoot a rifle, fish, and appreciate nature. One very important lesson he taught me remains with me to this day.

Luis, María, Fico, and I had finished our dinner when Papa came in looking for a box of razor blades. Luis excused himself for neglecting to order the blades that morning and suggested that Fico or I go down to the pueblo to the corner bodega and buy the razor blades. Fico looked at me with eyes wide open. I knew he was afraid of the dark and hated to walk around the Finca's grounds at night—above all in the vicinity of the well. I wasn't afraid of the dark, so I volunteered to go. Luis gave me money for the razor blades and wrote down the brand name of the single-edge blades on a piece of paper. I put the piece of paper in the back pocket of my pants and ran out of the house into the night.

I ran along the path through the pine trees and cut through the almond grove. My shortcut took me close to the sealed well where Don Pedro had drowned himself a year before. I stopped short. The horrible, ghastly image of his bloated body in the well sprang into my head, and fear got the best of me. I knew death lurked there. I ran fast toward the gate of the Finca. But as I ran accross the open field where we played baseball, I saw what appeared to be a body lying on the ground close to home base. A shapeless mass. And for a second I thought I saw it move. I closed my eyes and dashed to the gate. I hesitated for a moment and thought of stopping at my own house and asking for help. But the thought of being wrong and then ridiculed by my brothers convinced me not to do it.

I kept running until I reached the bodega. My fright-stricken face prompted the store owner to chuckle and ask me if I had seen a ghost. "There are no such things as ghosts," I responded too quickly, not appreciating his teasing. With the razor blades in hand, I walked out of the store and braced myself for the trip back.

I slowly walked along the deserted road, past my family's house, and through the gate. As I passed the ballfield, I turned my head from the shapeless, dark hulk on the ground. But I couldn't resist looking at the body. It was a dead body for sure. I could see the head, the white shirt, the shoulders. The ghost of Don Pedro had come back from the dead to haunt me! And now it was moving! I ran for my life and didn't stop to look back.

I reached the house and ran up the kitchen stairs. Luis, Fico, and María were waiting for me. Sweating, trembling, breathless, I stood in front of them. They asked what had happened. Fico gave me a glass of water. Luis and María tried their best to console me. Papa walked into the pantry and asked what was wrong with me. Luis couldn't give him an answer. Papa asked Luis to take me to the living room once I calmed down. After a few minutes, Luis took me to where Papa was waiting, reading in his favorite chair. He asked me what was wrong and I told him that I had seen a ghost, a dead body—the ghost of Don Pedro back from the dead to haunt me.

Hemingway immediately became alarmed. He had not forgotten the death of Don Pedro either, and the possibility of someone else killing himself on his property was not too far-fetched. He assured me that Don Pedro had died months ago and was buried. Then he stood up and took me by the hand. I didn't want to go with him, but I didn't want to show fear in front of him. We went out the front door and walked down the wide terrace steps. Chattering nervously, I told Papa that I hadn't been scared to run down to the bodega in the dark, but then I'd found myself in front of the well and the death of Don Pedro came to mind. And when I'd seen the body on the ground I'd panicked.

We walked the same path I had taken earlier. As we got closer to the baseball field, I started to tremble in my shoes. I clung to his big hand tightly. But then, embarrassed by my cowardice, I let go of it.

Papa put his arm around my shoulder. "Take it easy. What's the matter, muchacho? If you don't get a hold of yourself, you won't be able to show me where the body is." As we walked closer to home base, he said, "What you see is not what you think. Fear and imagination are playing a trick on your eyes."

I pleaded with him to believe me.

"Come!" he said, and I felt his heavy hand on my shoulder. He took me by the hand and we walked closer to the lifeless mass. I closed my eyes tight. "Open your eyes. What do you see at your feet?"

Slowly I opened my eyes, blinking several times. There at my feet was nothing more than a large guano leaf.

"This is the ghost in the darkness that was going to kill you of fright?" he joked. "The moment I saw it, I knew what it was."

"I'll move it away," I said angrily, embarrassed.

"No, leave it there," Papa said, explaining that a couple of weeks earlier Fico's father had asked for his permission to come and collect guano leaves from the ground. He said that tomorrow morning I would have been surprised and baffled by the disappearance of the dead body, and for the rest of my life I would have been sure I had seen a ghost tonight. Looking into my eyes, he said, "What you learned tonight make sure you never forget, muchacho. It will serve as a lesson. Remember, don't run away from what frightens you. Confront your fears and put your mind at ease. If I didn't show you what really scared you, your fears would have controlled your life."

"I promise it won't happen again."

"That's exactly what I expect from you." Then, noticing my shame, he said, "Cheer up, muchacho. I know you're not a coward. I've seen you box, and you never show fear. Always surprise your opponent. Do not let him surprise you. Be alert!"

"I learn a lot from you. You're always teaching me how to box. You take me fishing, and you said you'll teach me to shoot, and . . . "

"Slow down, take it easy, slow down! One thing at a time. You're not ready yet. Besides, I just gave you a K.O., con la izquierda y fácil [with the left and easy]." He smiled and gently tapped my chin with his left.

As we walked back to the house, his hand on my shoulder, I looked back toward the sealed well. Death was no longer there.

A couple months after the ghost incident, Luis resigned his position at the Finca to take a job that was closer to where he lived in Havana. Justo Pajé replaced him as majordomo. Justo was a dark-skinned Cuban with short, thinning hair, was of medium height and a little plump around the waist. Luis stayed the two weeks of Justo's trial period and in his poor Spanish dictated to me the list of responsibilities for the new majordomo.

From the moment Justo arrived, I knew he was trouble. After putting up a dutiful front for several weeks for el caballero, as he referred to Hemingway, Justo showed his true colors to the staff. He strolled through the house with an air of superiority, thinking he was above the rest of us. In no time he had made himself enemies by imposing his will and demands on the rest of us. He made María's life miserable with his constant outlandish demands for breakfast, lunch, and dinner. He refused to eat the food we ate and wanted the same meals that she prepared for Hemingway. He delegated most of his responsibilities to Fico and me. He was afraid of the dark and hated being alone in the Finca at night when the Hemingways were away, so he would ask Fico and me to keep him company, which amused us to no end.

Justo and Fico hated each other from the moment they met. The first mistake Justo made was to have Fico wash the delicate china. Fico's carelessness proved disastrous, and after several broken pieces Justo gave up on him. With me he resorted to a different tactic. He said he would train me as his right-hand man. But I knew he was just lazy and neglectful and wanted to unload more of his responsibilities onto me.

But I willingly took on new duties. I was curious about how things were cared for around the house, especially the hunting trophies. And as I learned to care for them and to perform other tasks, I appreciated the Finca even more. The times Papa saw me cleaning an animal head he would talk to me about it—what species it was, when and where it was shot, and what caliber rifle was used. He would describe the event in great detail. I listened carefully and I listened well, because to me that was my school, home, my paradise.

A TIME OF WAR

Before the summer of 1942 was over, more than thirty ships had been attacked by German submarines off the Cuban coast. Hemingway, restless and wanting to be involved, managed to convince personnel at the American embassy in Havana to allow him to patrol the Cuban waters in the *Pilar*. But before those efforts got under way, he became involved in an intelligence service operation spying against Falangists in Cuba. In August of that year, Spruille Braden, the new American ambassador to Cuba, recruited Hemingway and secured financial support to get the spying efforts under way. The covert operation originally known as the "Crime Shop" by embassy personnel was later changed to the "Crook Factory" by Hemingway.

There were a couple hundred thousand Spanish residents in Cuba at the time, and a small percentage, known as the Falangists, were thought to be sympathetic to the Nazi cause. Hemingway enlisted Basque priests, prostitutes, bartenders, jai alai players, and other Havana sorts for the effort. Cuba's proximity to the United States and its international population was strategically ideal for both sides. During that year, numerous German military and naval intelligence officers had arrived on the island as Spanish nationalists. It was rumored that the Falangists had provided the Germans with the false documentation in order to enter Cuba. The Crook Factory's mission was to spy and report on the known Falangists and "smoke out" any German spies in Havana. Though the Crook Factory was thought by some to be an absurdity, a joke, or simply an excuse for Hemingway to obtain fuel for the *Pilar,* Hemingway felt he was doing a good, legitimate service for the war effort.

Gustavo Dúran was called in by the American embassy to take over the Crook Factory operation and give Hemingway the opportunity to prepare the *Pilar* for her upcoming sea patrols. Dúran had commanded Loyalists forces during the Spanish Civil War and met Hemingway during that time. The two men shared a common ideal and became fast friends. However, shortly after Dúran took over the Crook Factory, Hemingway and some of the operation's inner circle felt that Dúran had lost his courage and had a different agenda and ideals from them. Hemingway and Dúran's friendship went sour as fast as it had begun years ealier in Spain.

After Hemingway's brief, eight-month involvement with the Crook Factory ended in April 1943, Martha Gellhorn left the Finca for a *Collier's* assignment to report on the submarine wars in the Caribbean. She had grown frustrated by Hemingway's comings and goings at all hours of the night and was more than happy to escape the mayhem. After she left, Hemingway kept himself busy by assembling a crew and patrolling off the north coast of Cuba in the *Pilar* looking for German U-boats.

I remember the conspiratorial, exciting feel of those war years—one evening in particular early in the summer of 1943. Hemingway returned from Havana with jai alai players Elmuar and Paxtchi, who were frequent guests at the Finca, and a man from the American embassy whom I'd never seen before. I had watched from the terrace as Juan and Hemingway drove up in the stationwagon. The others arrived separately. They unloaded three large tanks from the stationwagon. Hemingway left the group and came up to the house. Juan and the rest of the men stayed by the garage talking. I walked over to them and offered my help. Juan was glad for the offer. He had an ulcer and tried to avoid physical labor. I greeted Elmuar and Paxtchi and said "buenas noche" to the americano, who responded in fluent Spanish.

The men—who were obviously very drunk—discussed, with some difficulty, how to get the heavy, gasoline-filled tanks from the garage to the clearing down the hill where the gardeners had dug a hole earlier in the day. Fuel was scarce in Cuba because of the war and had to be severely rationed. Burying the tanks was one way of hiding the gasoline Hemingway had acquired for his patrols using his connections and with American embassy funds.

The men agreed that were two options for lowering the tanks to the clearing. One, they could lower the tanks one at a time down a steep hill of exposed roots, vegetation, loose soil, and several trees. This way would save time, but, considering the drunken state of the men, it would also be extremely dangerous. Two, they could carry the tanks one at a time along a narrow path around the hill. This would take longer and require a lot more effort, but it would be much safer. The men, not thinking very clearly, decided they would lower the tanks down the hill.

We found a thick, rusty old chain in the toolshed and fastened it to one of the tanks. Elmuar and the man from the embassy held the tank by the chain from the top of the hill while Paxtchi and I guided the tank to the bottom. Little by little, we inched our way down the slope. Everything seemed to be going well. Then the old chain snapped. Elmuar and the other man fell backward, the loose half of the chain in their hands. Paxtchi and I managed to step out of the way. The tank rolled down the slope, gaining speed.

Reacting—not thinking—I ran after the tank. I had no idea how I was going to stop it, but I somehow caught up to it and managed to grab a hefty branch from the ground and wedge it under the rolling tank. Fortunately, the branch then wedged itself between two trees and the tank stopped rolling.

The men ran down the hill asking if I was hurt. "Muçhacho estas loco," the American said to me. "If the tank had spilled, we would have never heard the end of it from Papa," Elmuar said, relieved.

After catching our breath, we maneuvered the tank down the rest of the hill, inch by inch, until reaching the ditch in the clearing. We pushed and rolled the other two tanks along the narrow path. It took forever this way, but it was certainly safer. While they buried the tanks, the men drank some more. By the time they finished late that night, they were a mess of dirt, sweat, and booze.

About a week later, late in the afternoon, I saw the same three men talking to Juan by the garage. They appeared to be under a lot of stress, pacing, talking loudly, and motioning with their hands. Juan called me over. Earlier that day Hemingway and the small crew had docked in Cojímar after a lengthy patrol, and Papa had sent the men for the much-needed tanks of gasoline. He told me that the men had come to dig out the tanks but had forgotten where they'd buried them, and Juan couldn't help them because he had not seen the location of the ditch. The gardeners, who'd dug the hole, had left for the day. The men had been frantically searching for some time. Did I know where the tanks were buried? I took them directly to the spot.

On another hot night, in early July that summer, I was startled awake by what I thought were burglars. With Papa and Martha away, and Justo in Havana, I had been sleeping in the library. I heard someone forcing one of the windows in the living room. I realized it was Papa, Paxtchi, and Winston Guest and opened the front door and let them in. The three men were bearded, dirty, and drunk. Paxtchi and Winston left and headed to Havana. Papa chose to sleep on the floor of the living room instead of a bed, saying it would be better for his land sickness. He and his crew had been at sea for more than forty days.

The next morning he awoke early. When I saw him, he was drinking gin in a glass. He asked for Justo, who had gone to Havana a couple of nights before and had not returned. There was no food in the house. (About a month earlier María had been instructed not to come until further notice.) I managed to get some eggs and bananas from the neighbor Don Julian. Papa drank his gin and ate the bananas. Concerned, I told him that a man from the pueblo was believed to have died after eating bananas and drinking rum. He assured me that he wouldn't die and said, "I know that you care a lot for me muchacho. Gracias."

Hemingway's arguments with Martha became more frequent and louder after the submarine hunt was over, and once it was she returned from her Caribbean assignment. He listened closely to the war news on the radio and read newspapers from the States and Cuba. He was slowly but surely bringing the war to himself.

On September 20, 1943, Martha left for New York to cover the war in Europe for *Collier's*. Alone at the Finca over the following months, Hemingway drank more heavily, grew a long beard, and gained weight. In the spring of 1944, he decided to leave for Europe himself. He arrived in England on May 17, 1944, but soon after arriving in London he was in an automobile accident and was for the first—but not the last—time pronounced dead by the world press.

When I heard the news on the radio, something inside me told me Papa Hemingway was still alive. It was Mancebo, the postmaster, who later obtained more reliable news and confirmed my intuition, telling me that Hemingway was indeed alive and not seriously hurt. Mancebo then asked me if I knew who I worked for. He was the first to make me aware of Hemingway's international fame and reputation as a writer.

He told me about the novels Papa had written. Certainly I knew that he was wealthy and had lots of friends, but I had not realized the magnitude of his fame until then. I was very proud to know someone like Ernest Hemingway. He was a friend, and now he was my hero.

Even with Martha and Papa away, life in the Finca went on as usual. Justo was losing his fear of the dark and began to guard the house by himself. Fico and I didn't have to sit with him at night anymore. But I guarded the house alone the nights Justo went to Havana and got drunk, often not returning until a couple of days later. While the cat's away, the mice will play—and Justo took complete advantage of the situation. Because I missed so much school when I stayed to guard the Finca in Justo's absence, I barely passed the eighth grade. So I stopped attending school. There were not many employment opportunities in San Francisco de Paula, and I knew that soon I would need a job to help my parents out.

I did not mind guarding the house all alone. Papa had taught me to confront my fears, and I was proud to be able to do so. During those nights alone at the Finca, I read the *Havana Post* and *El Pais* for details of the war and looked for anything that was written about Papa Hemingway. María left for good because there was no need for a cook, as did the maid.

In early October of 1944, the radio announced the threat of a category 3 hurricane. What came to be known as "the Havana Hurricane of 1944" developed over the southern Caribbean sea on October 12. On the 17th it reached its full force and struck Pinar del Río, the western most part of the island.

As soon as Justo heard the hurricane news he fled to Havana. Left to guard the Finca by myself, I asked Pichilo to help secure the doors and windows with the wooden storm panels Pancho had for such an emergency and which were stored in the garage. My father and brothers came up to the Finca to help, along with Pancho and Pichilo. In the pouring rain we secured the panels. I then locked the dogs in the basement of the main house, and Pichilo and I gathered the hens and roosters and placed their cages in the pool changing stall. We also moved the dovecote, which had more than 150 pigeons, to the basement of the house. When we were done, Pancho and Pichilo rushed to be with their families. My father urged me to come home and ride out the storm there, but I told him that I had to take care of the Finca.

As nightfall came, I peeked through cracks in the storm panels and windows and witnessed the devastation around me. Trees were being uprooted. One column from the pergola fell but, fortunately, missed the house. All alone in the big house, a sense of panic welled up in me as I thought of my family. I wanted to leave the Finca and get to them.

I waited for what seemed an eternity until the winds had subsided enough for me to venture out. I left the Finca through the kitchen door, the only door not bolted tight. It was more difficult than I thought to run in the wind and rain and navigate around the debris and fallen trees. As I reached the pine path, a gust of wind lifted me off the ground and pushed me forward several feet. I fell hard on my left shoulder and tried to hold on to whatever was around.

Muddy and scratched, I finally reached the gate. There I saw that the massive mamey tree had fallen. My heart sank. Before the storm my father had been very concerned that the large tree in front of our little house would fall and destroy our home. As I got closer, I saw that the tree had fallen on the Finca's gate and damaged both columns. I forced myself between a gap in the fence and reached my house. There I had to squeeze through a gap under the kitchen door. To my relief, everyone was safe. My father angrily scolded me for leaving the safety of the Finca. He told me that this was only the beginning and not the full force of the hurricane and forbade me to leave the house. Torn between my family and my responsibilities at the Finca, I disobeyed my father and crawled out of the house the same way I'd come in.

At the Finca I ran from room to room placing buckets under water leaks. As the buckets filled, I flushed them down the toilet in Hemingway's bathroom. A large branch from the ceiba smashed the roof above Martha's room, dumping several inches of water on the floor. Then the floorboards cracked, sending the water down to the basement. The rest of the house was spared from severe water damage.

My father had been right. The full strength of the hurricane struck San Francisco de Paula the next day, October 18, with incredible fury. Winds reached 165 miles per hour. The destruction on the central-western part of Cuba was unbelievable. In the pueblo, trees were uprooted, animals drowned. "Death, misery, and hardship is what a hurricane brings to the poor," my father said to us teary eyed as he appraised the damage to our little house. But we had been the lucky ones in the pueblo. We only lost the kitchen's zinc roof and a section of one bedroom.

Justo returned to the Finca three days later. He was nervous that Dr. Kholy, who oversaw the Finca when the Hemingways were away, would find out that he was not there during the storm. I never said a word about his absence, but someone else must have.

Don Julian Rodríguez, Hemingway's neighbor to the southeast, suffered terrible damages to his property and livestock. Don Julian was not insured, and the losses ruined him financially. (Not long after the hurricane, he became very ill and died. Sometime later Hemingway purchased a couple of parcels of land from Doña Pilar, the widow, who was in desperate need of money.) But the Finca Vigía was insured, and the insurance company compensated Hemingway for the damages to the house and property. Dr. Kholy asked Justo to take inventory of the damages on the house and property. As usual, Justo passed off his responsibility to me.

The pergola in the terrace had to be repaired, as did the columns at the front of the house and those at the gate. Trees had to be replanted. Inside, Martha's room suffered the most damage in the house. The water leak from the damaged roof ruined the Philippine matting, and the cracked floor had to be repaired. The restoration of the Finca began a few weeks after the storm and took a couple of months to complete. Throughout, I made myself accessible to Dr. Kholy and the workers in case they had questions regarding the restoration, but I also hung around simply out of curiosity to know what was being replaced and how. After all, the Finca was my home, too.

PAPA COMES HOME

In March of 1945, Ernest Hemingway returned to Cuba from Europe. Justo, Fico, and I were waiting for him in front of the house when he cheerfully stepped out of the stationwagon, clearly happy to be home. Looking fit, he had shaved the long beard he had when he left and now wore a mustache. He greeted all of us, warmly shaking our hands and smiling. He joked with Fico, telling him that he'd gotten taller but was still skinny and noted that Justo seemed heavier. To this, Justo sucked in his stomach. "You've also grown and gotten strong," he said, smiling at me. I was glad to see him back at the Finca.

The following morning, I arrived with the mail. Justo was in the kitchen preparing Papa's breakfast. He told us that Hemingway was going to spend most of the day in Havana. Justo took the breakfast tray, mail, and newspapers to the bedroom, trying very hard to impress Hemingway with his attentiveness. Justo's absences had been called to Hemingway's attention by Dr. Kholy. Hemingway's forgiveness of Justo's irresponsibility and incompetence baffled me.

Around midday, Juan drove up to the semicircular driveway and waited by the car. I was playing with one of the cats by the cistern. Justo opened the front door of the house and Papa walked out wearing a pair of slacks, a white guayabera, and moccasins—no socks, as was his custom. He carried a drink in his hand and took a sip from the glass as he walked over to me. He'd been watching me play with Big Goats from the living room.

"Big Goats and Fats have gotten very big," he said. "Soon they'll want to fight. They don't play together anymore." I told him that they're both good fighters and that Big Goats had already confronted Boise, their father.

Justo interrupted, nervously saying that I was keeping el caballero from his engagements in Havana. Hemingway assured him that I was not keeping him. He said that he had no pressing engagements and that there was no rush. Juan had been listening to the conversation and walked closer to us, looking at Justo in the eyes. He didn't care much for Justo and made no attempt to hide it. A couple of times Juan had intervened when he thought Justo had been unfair with Fico and my chores, which irritated the majordomo.

Justo walked closer to the cistern and tried to caress Big Goats, who, in response, hissed and jumped down from the cistern and ran away. We all laughed. Justo became defensive, saying, clearly insulted, "He prefers René's rough lumberjack hands to my soft caresses." Juan warned him to be careful because he would have to answer to him. Hemingway said nothing. He looked at me with a faint smile and headed toward the car. Juan and Justo followed. Hemingway said something to Justo before driving away. Justo walked back up the steps, looked at me hard, and went inside the house, all without saying a word.

The next day Juan arrived unusually late in the afternoon. I met him in the pantry. He was sitting, sipping café. "Papa is going to give Justo another chance, and he's also giving all of us a raise." Juan also told me that Hemingway was in love and that in a couple of weeks we would get to meet her. "He wants everything to be perfect around the house."

It was only then I realized that Martha Gellhorn was not coming back. A new woman was coming to take her place at the Finca. Martha's belongings had been sent to Havana for storage after the hurricane and during the restoration of the Finca. They would now be shipped to her.

Justo walked into the pantry, ignoring Juan. He told me that Hemingway wanted to see me feed the cats. I took the tray with the food for the cats and went to the terrace, through the French doors of the dining room. There Papa was waiting for me. I called out Wiwi's name several times in a high-pitched tone. In a matter of seconds, about a dozen cats ran out from under the bushes and climbed down from trees and rubbed against our legs.

"I see Wiwi hasn't changed at all," he said, looking out to the grounds, "still prefers to hunt pigeons and miss his meal." Since he was a kitten, Willy, or Wiwi, as we called him, had ignored my call for food. Because he was always missing, his was the name we called the most, so his name meant "feeding time" to the rest of the cats.

The cats followed Hemingway and me through the French doors into their room. As they ate, Papa and I talked about them. I picked a chunk of meat from the tray and threw it in one corner and picked another chunk and threw it in the opposite side of the room. Big Goats immediately went for the first piece. Fats jumped for the second. "If I didn't do this, there would be no food left for the others," I said. "By the time they finish the chunks, the rest of the cats have finished eating the food. This way I also avoid a fight between them." I placed the tray on the floor dividing the beef among three bowls. The rest of the cats attacked the bowls and in a few minutes finished the food. In their respective corners, Big Goats and Fats were just finishing up their large beef chunks.

Picking up a small black-and-white bundle from the floor, Papa asked if I had named the new kittens yet. "This beautiful kitten we're going to give to Miss Mary when she comes," he said. "She's staying for good. I need a woman like her here at the Finca. She's beautiful, smart, and sweet. She can help us name the kittens."

Papa often told me to name the cats with a name that had a long *s* sound at the beginning or the end of the name. Papa said cats loved *s* and responded better to it. I enjoyed pronouncing the names of the cats in English, especially Big Goats and Fats. We spoke about the size and weight of the male cats as if they were boxers, speculating on which would win in a matchup. We shared a love for the animals. I enjoyed these quiet conversations with Papa.

At around this time my parents took in a fatherless boy named David Fernández, whose mother could not raise him by herself. Our little house grew crowded, and so with Hemingway's permission, I moved my belongings into the newly restored basement room in the Finca. It really was my home now.

MISS MARY

Since his return to Cuba, Hemingway had gone out almost every day to Havana to dine and meet with friends. But with Mary Welsh soon to arrive, a new cook was needed. Papa placed an ad in one of the Havana papers, and within a couple of days we had a response. Papa asked me to meet the man by the gates and escort him up to the house.

"I'm Ramón Wong. I'm here for the cook's job," he said in strongly accented, broken Spanish. Ramón was Chinese, about fifty years old, and of medium height and build. He had a good handshake, the kind that makes you comfortable and lets you know a person is straightforward and honest. Hemingway interviewed Ramón and was impressed with his references and hired him on a two-week trial basis. He then took Ramón to the kitchen and introduced him to Justo. After Papa left the room, Justo brushed Ramón aside and said that he was too busy and that I should show Ramón around. This was the beginning of an antagonistic relationship between the Finca's majordomo and cook.

On May 8, 1945, Miss Mary Welsh arrived at the Finca. A very pretty woman, with fair skin, short light hair, a petite frame, and a vibrant smile, she soon won the love and admiration of the staff. Papa had hired a young girl who was a distant relative of Reymundo, the deaf gardener, to be her maid and another girl, Pilar, to teach her Spanish. He also hired a hairdresser and manicurist, Lily, who came every Wednesday morning and washed Mary's hair with rainwater collected in the cistern.

For a short time after Mary's arrival, Hemingway did not write. He woke up late, for him (at 7:00 A.M.), and spent most of the day reading with Mary by the pool. He gave her the black-and-white kitten, and she took it everywhere with her in her gardening basket. She named it Spendthrift, eventually shortening its name to Spendy.

In her early days at the Finca, Mary spent most of her time learning from the gardeners the Spanish names for the plants and flowers. She practiced her Spanish with all of us. She also liked to help Ramón in the kitchen, and in the process she learned to cook several Chinese dishes. Mary also visited my house and met my family. She took a special liking to Nilda and invited her up to the Finca to play with Spendy, talk, and work in the garden. She thoroughly enjoyed my nine-year-old sister's company. Nilda was full of questions and charm. Later on those days, she walked my sister home and spent time talking with my mother. She also made friends with Josefa Guerra, a talented seamstress who had a small shop not far from the Finca.

Mary adjusted to her new life at the Finca Vigía and worked hard to understand all the cultural differences. It could not have been easy to come to another country and learn a new language and live in a house that still had the furnishings and presence of her predecesor. Martha Gellhorn's photograph hung on a wall of their bedroom for quite some time before it was taken down.

In early June of 1945, Jack Hemingway came to the Finca straight out of a six-month detention in a German prison camp. Papa could not have been happier. He orchestrated a homecoming reception that involved the old gang from the pueblo and fireworks.

Bumby was just the same—respectful, happy, and full of life. No one would have ever thought he had just arrived from a prison camp. He was a little thinner, but he still looked strong. He spent the summer playing tennis, swimming, and reading. A couple of times he and I went trout fishing on the San Juan River in Matanzas. We had a friendly competition over who could catch more fish—Bumby with his artificial lures and flexible rod or me with my "Cuban tricks," as he referred to my real frogs, worm lures, and makeshift rod. Patrick and Gregory joined us when they came for their summer vacation.

On June 20 Mary was to travel to Chicago to finalize her divorce from her second husband, Noel Monks. Juan showed up to drive her to the airport, but Papa insisted that Juan sit in the backseat and let him drive so to avoid any possible problems with the striking Havana chauffeurs. It had rained earlier in the day, and the road to the airport was slippery. Hemingway, who had been drinking, lost control of the car and went off the road into a ditch. Papa sustained injuries to his head, ribs, and knees. Juan had only minor bruises. But Mary, who had been in the front seat, went through the windshield, resulting in multiple lacerations to her face that required plastic surgery.

For the next couple of months, Papa Hemingway was very caring toward and concerned over Mary. Once she had healed and her divorce was final, Papa and Mary got married in an unpretentious ceremony in El Vedado, Havana, on March 14, 1946. Now officially the lady of the Finca, Mary was able to plan and organize the household to better fit *her* needs.

AFTER WAR, PEACE

During the spring of 1946, life in the Finca was running smoothly. Mary liked her new maid Marta, and Papa Hemingway was hard at work early every morning. Justo was working well and not causing any problems. Ramón had been with us for over a year, and Fico had learned much from him and was also behaving himself. There was even a certain peace between Justo and Ramón. Justo simply didn't address Ramón, and Ramón couldn't have cared less. He performed his job with expertise and was given constant praise by Papa, Mary, and their dinner guests.

Then everything changed. Early one morning, I noticed that Justo was particularly agitated, pacing back and forth around the house. I went into the kitchen to see if there had been a confrontation with Ramón, but Ramón and Fico were going about their business as usual, unaware of Justo's agitated state. By lunchtime Justo was a bomb ready to explode.

Hemingway and Mary were swimming in the pool when Justo went into the kitchen to confront Ramón, who was slicing lettuce. "Today is the day!" Justo said defiantly, following it up with a crude derogoratory comment about Ramón's manhood. "We're going to see who leaves and who stays."

Ramón continued slicing the lettuce, ignoring Justo. But after Justo fired off another insult, Ramón banged the knife on the counter and faced Justo, ready to fight. He took a martial arts stance, eyes serene and alert. Justo turned and ran down the kitchen steps and outside.

Fico and I had some difficulty restraining Ramón, who wanted to end the feud once and for all. This is how we learned that Ramón was a martial artist.

From the first day Ramón began working at the Finca, he proved himself to be a respectable, honest, hardworking man. He didn't drink and was never late or absent. He spent his free time downstairs in his room or at the Chinese laundromat in the pueblo, where he talked with the proprietors for hours and where his old school friend worked. In the year we had known each other, Ramón and I had become good friends. I often accompanied him when he went to the pueblo. So I was very sad that day when Ramón told us he would be leaving after he'd cooked dinner and spoken with Papa and Mary. He said he couldn't take Justo's hostility anymore.

Papa and Mary ate their lunch completely unaware of the morning's excitement. But at some point during the meal, Justo went into Hemingway's study, where he took a handgun from the closet and hid it under his jacket before returning to the kitchen. There, Fico, Ramón, and Marta were cleaning and preparing their own lunch when Justo threw open the kitchen door and pulled the gun out, pointing it at Ramón. Instead of retreating, as Justo expected he would, Ramón grabbed a large kitchen knife and confronted him.

Terrified, Justo turned and ran out of the kitchen into the dining room, where Papa and Mary were finishing their meal. Fico, Marta, and I held Ramón back in the kitchen and begged him to wait for Papa or Mary to settle this. I then went out to the dining room and saw that Hemingway had disarmed Justo.

"You're fired! Take your things and go!" Papa screamed at Justo and called me over. I didn't see Mary. She must have left the room. "René will accompany you to the gate to make sure you leave." He told Justo to give me all the keys to the house and warned him that if he ever saw him around the Finca, he would shoot him on sight. He then ordered Justo to wait for him in the living room and went into his workroom. He returned and handed Justo a check.

When Justo went to collect his belongings, Papa whispered to me, "Be careful. Walk him all the way to the bus stop and don't leave until he gets on the bus. I think the syphilis has made him loco."

I met Justo outside by the front steps of the house, and we walked without saying a word. At the bus stop in the Carretera Central, he turned to me and said, "Today was my turn to lose. Adios muchacho. Thanks for all the help you have given me." He got on the bus. That was the last time I, or anyone else in the Finca, saw or heard of Justo Pajé.

On my return, Papa met me as I walked through the gate and up toward the house. He said, "After sending you out with Justo, I became worried. Do you think he might come back?" He was concerned. I told him that Justo left me all his keys and that I had made sure the gate was locked. Once inside the house, Papa went to the kitchen and convinced Ramón not to leave, assuring him that Justo would not be back to bother him.

Later that afternoon Papa and Mary returned to the house after another swim in the pool and found in the living room the ice bucket I had filled with ice and the cocktail mixer ready for martinis. I had set the table for dinner and had waiting in the pantry a variety of chilled wines. Mary smiled and complimented me on the table setting. She asked if I could handle serving dinner to a larger party, the only responsibility I wasn't familiar with. I told her that I would try my best.

"Don't worry. I can give you some pointers," she said. "Papa and I spoke about this while we were swimming. I'd feel very happy if you took the majordomo position, but Papa thinks you're very young and doesn't want to give you too much responsibility too soon."

I was disappointed to hear that Hemingway thought I was too young for the position. After all, my brothers Heliodoro and Luis were already working full-time jobs and contributing to the household. But over the next two days, I made sure Justo wasn't missed at all. And everything hummed along. In addition to my usual duties of picking up the mail and feeding the cats and dogs, I served the meals and took inventory of food, wine and liquor, and household supplies. Two warehouses in La Habana Vieja, Casa Gallarreta y Cony and Casa Recal, were the monthly alcohol suppliers to the Finca Vigía, and from El Morro Castle, another warehouse in Havana, we mostly ordered the fresh chicken, pork, turkey, ham, steaks, bacon, butter, shrimp, and toiletry supplies. I knew exactly what had to be done and did it. But still I had no idea if I had the position of majordomo.

One morning after I served Hemingway his breakfast, he told me that they were planning to spend a couple of weeks fishing off Cayo Paraíso. "Are you alright staying alone in the Finca? You're not afraid of ghosts?" he joked. He then told me that of all the staff at the Finca,

Fico and I were the youngest. If I became majordomo, I would have subordinates twice my age. He said that he had spoken to the other members of the staff, and there was not one who didn't like me or who would be bothered by me being the head of the house. Papa said that even the *Pilar*'s captain, Gregorio, thought I should be given the opportunity. But Papa and Mary left on their trip without giving me the final word.

A couple of days later, Dr. Kholy paid an unexpected visit to the Finca. Papa had asked him to check up on the house. He was pleased that I was being considered for the position of majordomo. He shook my hand, hugged me, and patted my back with great enthusiasm. "If there is anything I can help you with, you know were to find me. Adios muchacho, and keep up the good work." He shook my hand again and left.

I was very excited after Dr. Kholy's visit. When I told my parents that I was being considered for the position, they became very excited. It would be great for me to work at the Finca and be so close to them.

Each night I checked the grounds, walking with Negrita and Mota, my two faithful companions. On the ninth night, at around 1:30 A.M., the dogs became agitated. Someone was outside the house. The dogs didn't bark, but they paced back and forth, so I knew it had to be someone they recognized. I got out of bed and put on my pants and shirt. From the library, where Fico and I were sleeping, I ran to the living room. I turned off the light at the front of the house and waited by the window.

A few seconds later, a car drove up. I turned the outside light on. Papa rushed out of the taxi, looking anxiously up to the house. "René, it's us! Take it easy! It's only us!" He said this several times. Then Mary got out of the cab from the other side.

Relieved, I opened the door and went to greet them. Hemingway paid the taxi driver and asked the man to close the gate when he exited the Finca. Papa told me that they had cut the trip short but had gotten in too late to notify Juan to pick them up.

We went into the house, where Fico and Ramón were waiting for us. After seeing all was well, Fico, Ramón, and Mary excused themselves and went to bed. Then, visibly concerned, Papa asked me for the rifle I had been aiming at them when they got out of the taxi. I told him that I didn't have a rifle with me because I knew there had been no danger. I explained how the dogs had been restless but didn't bark, and how I knew it was someone familiar to them. I then took him to his study and showed him where I had hidden the key to his closet, where, since the incident with Justo, he kept the firearms locked. It was on the first shelf under the first book on the left side of the bookcase under the buffalo head. I unlocked the closet doors and showed him that the guns were all there exactly as he had left them. He smiled and took his boxing stance and threw a couple of light jabs at my jaw, gently tapping it. I took the same stance and pretended to evade his jab. Papa had played this game with me ever since I was a young boy. It was usually a sign that he was happy.

"You have passed one of the most difficult tests," he said. He then told me to put the key back in the same place. "In the morning, I will tell Miss Mary of the secret hiding place. It's late. Let's get some rest. Tomorrow morning don't worry about breakfast first thing."

I went to the library and picked up my shoes before going to my room in the basement. But before I could sleep, there was one more thing to do. I knew that the taxi driver hadn't closed the gate, so I walked out of the house, past the front of the garage, and along the pine path. I closed the gate and secured the lock. I was starting back to the house when I saw Papa coming down the pine path, his white guayabera giving him away in the darkness. In a quick motion, he hid behind one of the trees along the path. I was amused that he thought I had not seen him. He wanted to surprise me, I knew, and find out if I really was still afraid of ghosts.

Playing along, I hid behind a tree and took off my white shirt. In the night, my dark skin and black pants worked to my advantage. I became invisible. I ran stealthily around the tennis court and the swimming pool and cut through the almond grove, coming up right behind him. He worked his way down to the gate hiding behind the trees. I walked behind him without making any noise. Just behind him, I poked his back with my index finger and commanded him to halt. He calmly turned around and smiled.

He had also been concerned that the taxi driver wouldn't have closed the gate, but it was late and he didn't want to send me down to check. As we walked back up to the house, I thought of how calm he had been when I surprised him. Did I really catch him off guard, or did he know exactly where I was all the time? I never asked him.

With each passing day, I felt more comfortable serving lunch and dinner to the many house guests. My confidence grew. I knew there was not one thing I couldn't handle in the Finca. At the end of the month, Hemingway asked me to make a list of the employees who received monthly wages. He then sent Juan to the bank in Havana to withdraw the money, which I distributed before lunch. After lunch Papa asked to see me in his room.

"This check is for you." He handed me the check and smiled. "From now on you earn a man's wages." I could see he was pleased. Feeling great joy and relief, I shook his hand and thanked him. "Congratulations, René. I expect you will never let me down," he said, looking into my eyes. "It's settled then," Papa said and smiled.

At age seventeen, I was the majordomo of the Finca Vigía, a job I would come to hold and love for fourteen years.

OLD FRIENDS

In April of 1947, Patrick and Gregory Hemingway arrived at the Finca to spend their Easter vacation with us. Patrick had arrived first, since he was studying for the Harvard College Board Exams, and Gregory came directly from Canterbury School. Both boys were happy to see me as the Finca's new majordomo. We had known each other for years and played baseball, boxed, and fished together during their long summer visits.

Mouse and Gigi wanted to fish at the San Juan River in Matanzas, where we had been successful with trout on their last visit. On the morning of our fishing trip, Papa, concerned about Patrick's strange, nervous behavior, asked me to keep a close eye on him. "There is something wrong with him," he whispered in my ear, "but I don't know what it is."

The day turned out to be a disaster. The fish were not biting. Patrick, jittery and restless, kept moving to different spots on the river hoping to find better luck. He lost two tackles in the process, which aggravated him even more. Late in the afternoon, Gigi and I were ready to call it a day, but Mouse wanted to stay longer and wait for the stars to come out. He had been reading an astronomy book and was eager to study the constellations from the Cuban vantage point. We tried to persuade him to leave with us (nightfall wasn't for another couple of hours) but resorted to coercion to finally get him into the stationwagon. We had Juan park the car closer to where we were and then told Patrick he should sit in the car and wait for the sun to go down. Juan kept the engine running, so when Patrick got in the car

Gigi and I got in after him on either side, trapping him in the middle, not giving him an opportunity to escape.

Back at the Finca, Patrick told me he had a headache and asked me to get him a glass pot with boiled water for tea. I took a small aluminum pot filled with hot water to the guest bungalow. He appeared distressed and complained that the pot was dirty and began to argue with Ramón, who was not even present. I told him that it wasn't Ramón's fault, that it was my fault. I told him that I wasn't able to find a glass pot but assured him that the aluminum pot was brand new and clean. Hemingway heard his son's complaints in the main house and came to the bungalow. Mouse apologized for being loud. He said he knew it was not Ramón's fault, but the water was dirty. He grew more and more agitated. Hemingway suggested Mouse to go to the main house and get medicine for his headache.

I had never seen Mouse behave that way. He had always been very courteous and respectful. I knew that something terrible must be wrong with him. Later, I learned that Patrick had had an automobile accident in Key West and banged his head. After the accident, he slept all night out on the lawn of the house on Whitehead Street. He also had been under a lot of pressure preparing for his college exams.

In Papa's workroom, Patrick seemed to calm down. He sat on the large wicker recliner, Hemingway next to him speaking softly and gently stroking his head. I prepared the bed, and Papa and I moved Mouse from the recliner to the bed. Papa asked me to call Dr. Kholy and ask him to come over as soon as possible. Dr. Kholy wanted to speak with him, so I went and stayed with Mouse while Papa spoke to the doctor.

"Today's fishing excursion wasn't worth the long trip. It was too hot and there was too much sun," Mouse said in a low voice. He then excused himself for his behavior. I told him that it was fine and that I had only seen him upset once before. It had been a few years ago, I reminded him, when he and Gigi had visited the Finca, when we all played baseball together and sometimes boxed by the almond grove. Patrick used to box a couple of rounds before going off to draw and paint by the cistern. One day a group of boys from the pueblo had come to challenge us. Usually we paired off by age or size, but there was a new boy named Felix Soza, a dark-skinned, tall, strong southpaw. He was about Patrick's height and age. Gigi wanted to box him, but we didn't allow it because Felix was much bigger. Gigi told Patrick there was a challenger for him, but Patrick refused to fight. Gigi then told Patrick that he would box Felix if he didn't.

As I told the story, I saw Patrick's eyes twinkle with remembered delight. "Yes, I remember now. He caught me with a hard left and knocked me to the ground." I then reminded him how, fired up, he had gotten up and proceeded to outbox Felix and how, when Patrick got him in trouble, Felix tried to tie him up in a clinch. Felix, trying not to fall, had lifted his legs in an attempt to keep his balance. But it looked like he was trying to kick Patrick with his knees.

Patrick laughed. He remembered that Papa had been watching the match from a distance and come closer to tell Felix to stop bucking with the knees. Poor Felix saw Papa coming and ran down the hill screaming, "Don Ernesto is going to hit me!" He ran with gloves and all. We chased him to get the gloves back, but the more he looked back the faster he ran, thinking we were going to trap him and bring him back to Papa. Felix reached La Carretera Central and ran inside his house. It took a while before we finally convinced him to give the gloves back. Papa later invited him to the house to reassure him that he had no intention of hitting him.

Patrick and I were both laughing when Papa entered the room and smiled. "I can see you are feeling better. Dr. Kholy will dine with us tonight and take the opportunity to examine you," he told his son. "He'll recommend something for your headache."

Later that evening, after his examination, Dr. Kholy advised that a neurologist examine Patrick. The following morning, even under the sedatives prescribed by Dr. Kholy, Patrick was irritable and nervous. Dr. Kholy consulted with a neurologist and they agreed that Patrick would be better looked after in a hospital. But Hemingway insisted that his son stay at the Finca and not be admitted to a hospital.

Over the next couple of days, Mouse's mental health deteriorated. Specialists from all over the island visited the Finca Vigía. At this same time Mary received news that her father was to have an operation, and she had to travel to the States. So Hemingway called on his close friends to help him keep vigil over his son. Dr. José Luis Herrera came to the Finca three or four times a week, and his brother, Roberto, and Simbad stayed in the library. And sometimes Elmuar also came to help. But when Father Don Andrés came in his black robes, Patrick went into an agitated, frantic state, screaming "Black Priest!" at the poor man. The name stuck with Don Andrés ever after.

We all took turns caring for Patrick in shifts, making sure he was not left alone. Mouse refused to speak in English and communicated in Spanish. He allowed only me to feed him, which I had to do with my hands because we thought it could be dangerous for him to use any kind of metal utensil. He called me his African brother.

Papa provided the best comfort he could for his son, and after several months of illness we began to see improvement. In July, Pauline, Patrick's mother, came to see him. By summer's end, Patrick was back to his old self, and Pauline returned to the Finca to accompany him back to the States, where he would continue his studies. A greatly relieved Papa Hemingway planned a farewell fishing trip aboard the *Pilar*. Mouse requested that I accompany them. We spent a great day fishing and feasting on Gregorio's cooking.

In October of that year, I was surprised when Papa asked me to pack a single suitcase for him. He usually traveled with a lot of luggage filled with changes of clothes and many books. He told me that he had to leave Cuba in a hurry. The Cuban government was arresting individuals suspected of assisting in an attempt to overthrow Dominican Republic's president Rafael Trujillo, and Papa had written several personal checks to support the effort. His friends Paco Garay and Manolo Del Campo Castro (no relationship to Fidel Castro) were also involved.

The Dominican revolution had its main base of operations in Cayo Confites and Cayo Romano, keys located north on the eastern part of Cuba near Nuevitas. As news spread of the arrests at the keys of more than 1,500 men, Hemingway got word to Gregorio Fuentes in Cojímar to dispose of his machine guns stored aboard the *Pilar.* Once far out at sea and in the dark of night, Gregorio hurled the weapons overboard. Shortly after Hemingway's departure, Cuban soldiers confiscated the hunting rifles at the Finca and took them to El Cotorro. Later they were moved to the house of a judge, where I had easier access in order to maintain them until they were eventually returned to the Finca.

Hemingway was fortunate when an American in Havana was accused and arrested of assisting the failed revolution, thus lifting suspicions from Papa. I suspect that Paco Garay, who had his share of influential friends in the Cuban government and in other high circles, somehow made the whole mess disappear. Even so, Hemingway remained in Sun Valley, where Mary joined him in October. The Hemingways did not return to Cuba until February of 1948.

ROYAL TREATMENT

It was a quiet Sunday afternoon in April 1948, warmer than usual for that time of year. Papa Hemingway read in his favorite chair in the living room, relaxed in his khaki-colored shorts, white short-sleeve guayabera, and favorite oversized moccasins and enjoying the remainder of a bottle of Château Margaux from lunch. It was my day off, and I was killing time arranging the magazine stand in the living room. After lunch Mary had gotten dressed and left with Juan, who had come in from Havana on his day off per her request. She and Papa had been invited to the Steinharts' house for an afternoon party. Papa refused to go, so Mary had gone by herself.

Frankie Steinhart was hosting a party in honor of his special guest, the Duke of Windsor. Edward VIII was on his way back to England after visiting several British outposts and enjoying several rounds of golf with friends in Havana. Mary was thrilled to have been invited. Over the years she tried hard to maintain good relations with the Steinharts. Despite Mary's pleas and several requests from Frankie Steinhart, however, Hemingway refused to attend the party. He was happy staying home and reading in the comfort of his favorite chair.

Not long into the afternoon, the telephone rang. I walked over to the pantry and answered it. Señor Steinhart was on the other end of the line. He asked to speak with Papa. Hemingway walked to the pantry and reluctantly took the receiver. He spoke to Steinhart and once again declined the invitation. Papa went back to the living room and continued his reading.

A few minutes passed and Frankie Steinhart called again, insisting that he speak with Hemingway one more time. After a couple of minutes on the telephone, Papa returned to the living room and took his seat. "Son of a bitch wants me to attend the party. It's a damn black-tie affair in the middle of the afternoon. And with this heat." Papa was irritated. He took a sip of wine.

Another few minutes passed and the telephone rang again. This time it was Mary on the line. She politely asked for Papa. Hemingway, not amused, walked over to the pantry and took the phone from me. I left the room. Shortly after, he came out, his face flushed. He walked over to the living room and sat down in his chair.

"Miss Mary is also insisting I go over. She says the Duke of Windsor wants to meet me." I asked him if he wanted me to get a suit ready for him. He told me not to bother, that he told Frankie and Mary that he was relaxing, reading, and enjoying his afternoon.

Sometime later the telephone rang again. This time there was a voice I did not recognize on the other end of the line. The man spoke a different sort of English and was very polite and proper. Papa walked to the pantry once more and took the receiver. This time he expressed surprise at the caller. The conversation was brief, quiet, and cordial. Hemingway walked back to the living room, running his hand through his hair, saying to me, "That was the Duke of Windsor."

Papa asked me what my plans were for the rest of the afternoon. I told him that I had no plans. "René, do you mind coming with me?" I told him that I would get a suit ready for him to wear and that I would change into my Philippine serving jacket. "No, René, we are going as we are," he said in a calm determined voice. The telephone rang again, Steinhart calling to say that he was going to send a car over. Papa said that it wouldn't be necessary. He would be there in a few minutes.

Back in the living room, Papa looked at the liquor tray and said, "René, gather all the necessary things to make the martinis. We're taking our own liquor, and you will mix my drinks. I don't trust that son of a bitch Frankie. He may just try and poison me today in front of everyone. Besides, no one makes a dry martini like you," he added with a wide smirk. I didn't know if he was joking or being serious about Steinhart poisoning him. He then went to his bathroom and combed his hair and washed his face. When he came back to the living room, I had gathered some thinly sliced onions and olives for the martinis. Papa took a bottle of Gordon's Gin and I the onions, olives, and dry vermouth, and together we left the house from the kitchen.

We walked alongside the fence that ran between the Steinhart property and the Finca. Conspicuously, we entered Steinhart's property from the rear. The party was in full bloom. There were guests in the main house, by the pool area, and throughout the gardens. Señor Steinhart had gone to every expense to accommodate and impress his royal guest. He had hired an extra staff of bartenders and servers and rented tables and chairs.

"I told Frankie from the beginning that if he wanted me here, I would come as I am. It is too damn hot to wear a suit," Papa said to me looking down at his shorts and moccasins. Sitting down in a chair by the pool, Hemingway stood out from the other male guests, who all wore tuxedos or elegant suits. At that moment it dawned on me that I was also severely underdressed for the occasion. I had forgotten that I was wearing a short-sleeve white guayabera, a pair of black slacks, and shoes with no socks. But I was not the world-famous writer. The headwaiter quickly approached us carrying a white serving jacket meant for me.

"Is that for him?" Papa asked, confronting the man in a loud tone. "If you are going to make him wear that, then you better bring one for me as well. And make sure mine is a large one, because I'm a big guy." He grabbed the jacket from the man's frozen grip. "I don't think this jacket will fit me," he said as he slid his left arm into the sleeve of the jacket. Papa had a difficult time getting his right arm into the other sleeve. The jacket was very snug on him. "I told you that I'll need a larger jacket," he said as he moved his arms exaggeratedly and raised his voice. Frankie Steinhart motioned to the head waiter to leave us alone. Hemingway took off the jacket and handed it to the terrified waiter. "Get this rag out of here and bring us a cocktail mixer, an ice bucket, and a table where we can mix drinks."

In about a minute's time we had a small table where we set the bottle of gin, the dry vermouth, the olives, and the onions. There was also an ice bucket with plenty of ice and a cocktail mixer. The waiter managed to ask Papa if he wanted anything from the bar.

"I doubt there is anyone here who can mix a martini like René," Papa replied. The waiter excused himself and hurried away. Papa looked at me and laughed. I mixed Papa a strong dry martini.

Frankie Steinhart walked over with the Duke of Windsor and other guests and introduced them to Hemingway. Papa shook their hands. Steinhart asked the waiter to bring drinks for the group. The Duke of Windsor said that he would have a martini like the one Hemingway was drinking.

I mixed more martinis for the group, just as strong as I had made Papa's. More and more guests came over to meet Hemingway, and they requested martinis. It wasn't long before the Duke of Windsor had taken off his jacket, loosened his tie, and rolled up his shirtsleeves. Then another guest followed, and another and another.

That June of 1948 Papa also met A. E. Hotchner for the first time. Hotchner went to the Floridita in Havana to interview Hemingway for a *Cosmopolitan* magazine article on the "Future of Literature." I remember how Papa and Roberto Herrera often told friends about the next time he met with Hotchner. Roberto was with Hemingway for that second meeting and helped Papa play a joke on Hotchner at the Floridita.

Papa had ordered a tray of cooked whole prawns for the table, along with Papa Dobles, the daiquiris named after Hemingway in the local bar. Papa grabbed a prawn and put it in his mouth whole—with head, shells, and intestinal tract. Roberto distracted Hotchner while Papa spat the mouthful into his napkin and took a sip from his drink. Roberto did the same, with Papa distracting Hotchner. Not wanting to be left out, Hotchner followed suit. But he struggled with the prawn in his mouth before taking several sips from his drink to swallow the mess. Even the waiters were in on the joke, discreetly supplying Papa and Roberto with fresh napkins whenever possible.

THE KILLERS

Papa and I shared a great love for nature and animals, and I always respected how he provided a safe and comfortable haven for his pets and showed affection for each and every one of them.

Uncle Buffie, the oldest of the Finca cats, passed away one night in the early summer of 1948. I found him the next morning curled up in the corner where he slept. I waited for Papa to finish his breakfast before I told him the news.

"I was expecting it to happen any day now," he said sadly. He asked where I had buried the two dogs—Gang and Lane—who had died while he and Mary were in Sun Valley. I told him that I had buried them behind the dog pound under a mamoncillo tree where they used to sleep. "We need to find a good place to bury our cats. A sound place that no one would disturb and only we know about it. Have you thought of any?" I showed him a spot outside the entrance to the dining room where there was a small garden with roses and Mexican cactus. Behind the cactus there was enough room for a small burial ground. The spot is full of thorns and would discourage anyone from getting close. "This is an ideal place. No one would ever disturb these grounds," Papa said, satisfied.

I went to the gardeners' shed and got a shovel and a pick. I also found a couple of bricks to outline the grave. At Hemingway's request, before burying him I wrapped Uncle Buffie in an old copy of the *New York Times*. After the hole was covered over, we placed a cactus leaf on the grave and arranged the bricks. We solemnly shook hands and then went on about our business.

It was about this time that Papa and Mary were having the tower constructed. The four-story building was being built to house a new work studio for Papa, as well as to provide more space for books, fishing and hunting gear, and the growing family of cats. With the chaos of construction, Papa grew restless and preocccupied. He stared out his workroom window, pacing back and forth and from room to room. He couldn't read or write and grew increasingly irriated by the noise and dust. When he couldn't take it anymore, he had me call Gregorio at La Terraza and leave a message for him to prepare the *Pilar* for the following morning. He and Mary would go fishing for a couple of days to escape the mayhem.

But once home again, it didn't take long for him to grow restless. Mary, however, continued with her everyday activities and managed to ignore the workers, the noise, the grime. She tended her gardens and arranged flowers for the house. One morning she went out to the rose garden with her basket and her favorite cat, Spendy. After tending the gardens and back in the house, she noticed that Spendy hadn't followed her in. She began looking for the cat. Several of the workers stopped what they were doing and helped her with the search. Reymundo, the head gardener, and I joined in the search, hoping to cover a broader area. But still there was no sign of Spendy.

Mary, very upset, went into the house and blamed the aggressive brother cats, Big Goats and Fats, for little Spendy's disappearance. She told Hemingway that the two bullies had killed her cat. She also blamed a hoodlum yellow cat from the neighborhood and Shopsky, another of the male cats in the house. In the end she blamed all the aggressive male cats in the house, arguing and crying and pleading with Papa to take action against the culprits. Privately, I told Papa that it was unlikely for two rival cats to unite and kill a smaller one or even team up with a strange stray from the neighborhood to do so. The smaller cats didn't confront Big Goats or Fats. They ran and avoided confrontation. It would have been no different with Spendy.

Later that day, one of the mason workers on his way back from the pueblo found the lifeless body of Spendy by one of the gardens close to the small road leading to the gate. Several people had searched that area before and had not seen the body. Pichilo assured me the cat had not been there before when he'd looked. We concluded that Spendy must have been killed outside the Finca and thrown back over the fence. We knew that one of the closest neighbors had a pit bull they trained to fight and surmised that Spendy must have wandered into the backyard and been killed by the dog. Knowing the cat belonged to Mr. Way, the neighbor probably threw it back over the fence. They knew killing one of el americano's cats was definitely asking for trouble.

I returned to the house to tell Hemingway what I thought really happened. There Papa was consoling Mary. She was insisting on punishing the killer cats. They argued in English. I couldn't understand what they were saying, but my guess was that he probably defended Big Goats and Fats. Mary went to her room crying. He followed her but a few minutes later came out flush-faced and upset. "We won't be having lunch together," he said and then asked for a Tom Collins and a sandwich.

I presented my theory about Spendy's death to Papa. He told me that Mary insists it was Big Goats and Fats and accuses us of not caring at all for Spendy. She said we only like the fighting studs of the family. Hemingway said, still very upset, "She wants me to shoot them both." I felt the blood drain from my face. I couldn't speak. I excused myself and rushed to the pantry and prepared his drink and sandwich.

When I went to his room with his lunch, I found him holding his .22 caliber rifle. He looked at me solemnly, like an executioner who didn't want to carry out the sentence. I left the room and went outside to look for Big Goats and Fats. On the terrace I saw Fats lazily sunbathing on the floor. I picked him up and hid him in the cats' room. Then I searched around the grounds for Big Goats. I saw the yellow-striped hoodlum cat we called "the Stranger" and chased him off the Finca grounds into his house. I made the children of the house take him in, telling them there was a mad dog on the loose killing cats. The only one I needed to find was Big Goats. I had no idea were he was. I ran to the garage hoping to find him there. As I reached the garage I saw Papa, rifle in hand.

"Muchacho, what are you doing?" Hemingway said sternly, stopping me in my tracks. I had been looking for Big Goats, I told him, out of breath. I asked him to check Big Goats for traces of blood before shooting him.

I looked through his spectacles and into his eyes. I knew he didn't want to shoot them. I told him that I wouldn't come back to work later in the afternoon. "Please, if you are going to shoot them don't do it here. Take him farther away from the house," I pleaded, tears streaming down my cheeks.

"You care for them a lot," Hemingway said solemnly.

"We both do," I said. "You're their owner and I take care of them."

"I'm not a cold-blooded killer," he raised his voice. "I don't take any pleasure from killing my own cats. I love them as much as you do!" He cocked the gun looking straight at me.

"I'm going home," I said, and turned away.

"Esperate! Wait!" Hemingway commanded.

I turned around. Hemingway raised the rifle in the air and fired a shot, then another and another. He lowered the rifle and emptied out the remaining cartridges. He looked straight into my eyes and handed me the extra bullets. "Hold on to them until you think it is safe to load the rifle again." He cocked the rifle and aimed upward and tried the trigger. The rifle was empty. He walked over to the garage door and leaned the rifle against it.

We looked at each other for a while and didn't say a word. Then I turned and walked away. "Big Goats is waiting for you to bring his food!" Hemingway called after me. I turned around to look at him and saw Big Goats playing around Papa's feet, stroking his head and pressing his body against his moccasins. I ran back and picked up the cat and showed Papa that there was no blood on him. Not a single trace. Not even on his big *bigotes*!

"I know you were not lying. You have never lied to me," Hemingway said and looked into my eyes. "Get the food. He looks hungry. We better keep them out of sight for a couple of days, until Miss Mary calms down."

Days passed, and no one mentioned Spendy, or his death, again. I buried him in the cats' cemetery next to Uncle Buffie. For a while Mary didn't go down to the gardens. Instead, she had Pichilo pick the flowers and vegetables and bring them to the house. A few times I saw Papa take Sun Valley, a cuddly female kitten, to her room only to then see Marta let it out. I was bothered that Mary avoided eye contact with me and spoke as little as possible. She thought I had taken sides with Big Goats and Fats and that I didn't care for Spendy. Eventually, though, her anger subsided and we became friends again.

The construction of the tower dragged on into the fall. Hemingway and Mary went out in the *Pilar* as often as possible to avoid the chaos. But soon the fishing trips weren't enough, and they headed to Europe with plans to return once the tower was completed. So in the fall of 1948, they left on the *Jagiello* out of Havana harbor—destination Venice, Italy.

THE TOWER

Hemingway and Mary returned to the Finca in May of 1949. Juan drove them back from the port, the stationwagon filled with suitcases and boxes. Another trip had to be made with a small truck to pick up the rest of the luggage.

That afternoon after settling in, Papa and Mary relaxed in the living room, enjoying a couple of martinis before dinner. Papa congratulated me and Ramón on the work we'd done restoring the matting in the living room. He said it looked as good as new. In their absence Ramón and I kept ourselves busy by repairing the Phillipine matting that had suffered much wear and tear from foot traffic. Ramón suggested we use the long leaves of the pandamor tree. The biggest challenge was trying to get long, uniform strips from each leaf, which had a short stumpy thorn in the middle. I designed a small tool using four evenly spaced single-edge razor blades that spliced a leaf into even strips and at the same time trimmed away the thorn. Pancho, the carpenter, offered to make the jig for me in exchange for a bottle of rum. A fair trade, I thought.

Mary and Papa presented the staff with gifts from their trip. Papa gave me a Swiss watch and Mary gave me a fine leather jacket. They often brought gifts to the staff after a long trip. In Venice, Mary had also purchased suitcases, clothing, and fine china bordered in gold and embossed with an interesting emblem. She saw my intrigue as we unpacked the china and explained that she and Papa had designed this Hemingway crest and that it would go on all their possessions from now on. Mary told me that the emblem was made up of a line drawing of three overlapping mountains symbolizing the three mountainous places where Hemingway spent the happiest days of his youth: on the left Wyoming, in the middle Montana, and the right Idaho. Under the mountains was a Native American war shield, which represented the ancestry Hemingway believed he had. Under the war shield were the three horizontal stripes of a captain's rank Papa thought he deserved for his participation in two world wars. Pancho later made a mold of the crest and used a branding iron to brand the new suitcases and many other personal items.

Mary asked me why I had not moved the cats to their new home in the tower. I told her that it had been my intention to wait until Eduardo Rivero, the architect, officially handed the tower over to them. I had already fed the cats several times in their new space and told her that I thought they were used to it already.

"As of today you have our permission to move los gaticos to their new home," Papa told me, smiling. "Boise, Princessa, and the new kittens can remain inside the main house." The cats were then moved to the tower, and the room was cleaned and painted and made into a guest room.

Everyone eased back into their routines. Papa worked from early in the morning until about noon. Mary gardened and supervised the never-ending improvements and decorating of the house. The bookcases for the library had been completed while they were in Europe, so now she and I had the task of organizing and shelving the thousands of books scattered throughout the house.

The furniture for Hemingway's new studio in the tower was ready as well and had to be accommodated. Early one morning I helped him move his things from the workroom out to the tower. That morning I went on with my responsibilities around the house, but as I worked I missed the sound of the typewriter. The house felt empty, too quiet. I walked to his bedroom and stared at the corner by the large window where he had worked. His absence saddened me.

No more than an hour later, I saw Papa through one of the windows of the living room. He was carrying his typewriter, papers, and pencils. "Open the door," he said, almost in desperation. I helped him carry his things back to his workroom. "Please bring the rest of my stuff down from the tower," he said. Pleased, I returned with the items.

Back in his workroom, Papa was waiting for me. "Just leave everything on top of the bed. I will arrange it later." He walked over and stood in front of his typewriter, which he had put back on the same thick book on the top shelf. "I couldn't concentrate, or write. Something was missing. I felt trapped. I missed the sounds of the house, the view from my window, the sound of you sweeping the matting. I missed it all." He asked where Mary was and said that eventually he would have to break the news to her about the studio. It had been her project. "Now I want to get right back to work. Perhaps I can recuperate the lost time," he said with a worried smile. At the time he was working on *Across the River and into the Trees*.

I left the room and started to sweep the matting. In a few minutes, I heard the familiar click-clack of the typewriter.

MORNING'S JUICE

In the summer of 1950, Papa worked diligently—waking up earlier than usual and also finishing the day's work later. It was a very productive period of writing for him. He seemed happy and pleased with his work.

On one of those mornings, I walked into his room to ask him if he was ready for breakfast. "This morning I wish to have some of the canned fish Miss Mary bought in Havana, with two crackers, a slice of preserved apricot, and a bottle of cold juice," he said, smiling and motioning me to follow him over to the wastebasket in his workroom. He bent down and lifted out a small, empty cardboard box. Inside was the wine bucket with ice and an empty bottle of champagne. Mary and Hemingway had opened the bottle of champagne late the night before but were not able to finish it. He had finished off "the juice" this morning and wanted more. "The wastebasket is deep and conceals the bottle well," he whispered and smiled. "All I need to do is place an empty box on top. Only you, Boise, and I know about it. This is the juice I want to have this morning. Don't uncork the bottle in the pantry. Bring it here wrapped in a napkin. I will teach you how to open a bottle of champagne without making a sound."

The following morning I asked Papa if he wanted the same juice for breakfast. He decided on the more usual half-glass of grapefruit juice instead. I prepared breakfast and brought it to the room.

"You have a lot of money inside the top drawer of the desk," Papa said as he started on his breakfast. I walked over to the desk and opened the drawer. I told him that it was his not mine. "It can't be mine either," he said. I explained to him that when he went to Havana, most of the time he left money inside his pants' pockets or guayaberas, and before I had them washed, I made sure there was nothing left in the pockets. If I found money, I kept it in the drawer.

"How much do we have?" he asked with a happy look on his face. "Let's count it, muchacho. There's enough for both of us." I told him that I couldn't accept the money because I had not earned it. He insisted that half of it was mine. Papa was happy with the money windfall. "I never imagined it was there," he said laughing. I told him that my parents were going to wonder where I got the money. I had few expenses and didn't know what to do with the money.

"Don't you go out? Don't you like the movies. Don't you like girls?" Hemingway asked, a smirk on his face.

"Very much, but right now I want to stay away from them as much as possible," I said, embarrassed.

"Bad experience?" he asked.

I told him that I had fallen in love with a girl from the pueblo but then found out that she was seeing two other young men on the side besides me. My parents had known about it, and so did my brothers, but they were embarrassed to tell me. I guess I wasn't spending enough time with her. My father wanted to take me trout fishing on Sunday for a talk, I told Papa. He knew I'd been feeling down since I broke up with the girl.

Some days later, after Hemingway had finished his day's writing and was enjoying the cool waters of the pool, I brought him his first drink of the day. "How did the fishing go?" Hemingway asked as he swam toward me. I told him that we only caught four small trout and threw them back. "I can see you're still sad and upset. Did your father scold you?" He pulled himself out of the pool and I gave him the drink. I told him that my father advised me to fall in love with a girl who is a hard worker and a good person, like my mother. "Sounds like good solid advice," Papa said, taking a long sip.

I told him that my father had also given me permission to buy the colt I had been looking at and then asked for Papa's permission to graze the horse on the Finca grounds. "You don't speak to me about your problems," he said. "You're always helping everyone around here and don't look out for yourself. I'll buy you the horse as a present, since you wouldn't take the money."

Trueno was a beautiful colt—shiny black with a diamond-shaped white spot on the forehead and white coloring on the lower part of his legs. When I took the colt to the Finca, Papa came to see the horse. "Splendid beast," he commented.

After becoming the Finca's majordomo, I was able financially to contribute more to the household. The opportunity arose for my family to purchase three large lots in Reparto la Prosperidad, a section of San Francisco de Paula that was being developed. We needed to secure the three lots in order to build our family's homes, but we didn't have the necessary 2,000 pesos for the down-payment.

Earlier that week, Papa had invited my father and Luis up to the Finca on Saturday to watch the fight reel of Rocky Graziano versus Tony Sale. My father wanted to ask Hemingway for a loan, but I told him that I'd rather do it. I told Papa our situation and assured him that I would pay him back monthly from my wages. Without hesitation he wrote a check with an extra 500 in the sum in case it was needed. With that we were able to purchase the three lots on which we eventually built three homes.

That month, when it was time to pay the Finca staff, I omitted my name from the payroll list. Papa asked me why I had done it, and I told him that I wanted to start paying back the loan. He told me that I wouldn't be able to assist my parents now when they needed me most. "The loan is between you and me. I'll let you know when you have to pay me back." Papa never asked me for the money.

THE OLD MAN AND THE SIREN

Among the most memorable of the many, many houseguests at the Finca were the Ivanciches. Hemingway had met Adriana in Venice in December of 1948 and was immediately infatuated with the sultry eighteen-year-old beauty. He later met her mother, Dora, and brother Gianfranco. The Ivanciches were aristocratic, established, respected Venetians who had fallen on hard financial times after the father, Carlo, had been murdered by political rivals following the war.

The Ivanciches' arrival came just after Hemingway, working intensely, had sent off to New York the final galley proofs of *Across the River and into the Trees*. The immediate pressure had been lifted, but Papa remained nervous and anxious anticipating the arrival of the Ivanciches from Venice. Papa told me that Adriana was a beautiful girl full of life and charm and that she had been the inspiration for Renata in *Across the River and into the Trees*.

Hemingway had asked Mary to shop for him at El Encanto, one of Havana's finest clothing store, where she bought him new guayaberas, pants, shorts, and shoes. He wanted to look his best for the guests and also provide the best possible hospitality. So the staff worked hard to ready the grounds and prepare the bungalow for these important guests.

Gianfranco was the first to arrive in Cuba in the latter part of 1949. The carefree, handsome young man took up quarters in the former cats' room, which was now the newly restored guest room. He came with aspirations of becoming a writer and attempted to write in the guest room, the living room, and the fourth floor of the tower—always leaving a mess of crumpled papers behind but nothing written in his notebook. (He was tutored by Hemingway to no avail.) Nevertheless, he was an easy person to get along with. And since he was the visitor who stayed the longest at the Finca Vigía, after he left, the guest room became known as the "Venetian Room."

When Adriana and Dora arrived on October, 28, 1949, I saw immediately why Hemingway had been taken with this girl. Indeed, she was a beautiful, dark-haired, sultry siren. With her smiling green eyes and full lips, Adriana had no trouble conquering any man. I couldn't blame Papa for his schoolboyish behavior. She really was a sight to behold. She liked the attention she received from Hemingway—he spoke tenderly to her in Italian, French, or English—and flirted with him the way a schoolgirl flirts with an older professor. But to Hemingway's dismay, Dora never left her daughter's side. She walked behind Hemingway and Adriana like an armed escort, carefully watching their every move.

It wasn't long before his courtly behavior got him in trouble with his wife. Mary was smart and tolerant, but there was only so much she was willing to take right in front of her face and in her own home. On several occasions, late at night after dinner, Mary and Hemingway argued loudly in their bedroom. There were even several harsh arguments in front of the Ivanciches that involved spilled wine. At one point I heard Mary say she was going to leave him for good.

After a particularly loud argument, Papa walked into the pantry and asked me to prepare the bed in his workroom. "Miss Mary is good to me. She's very smart and I love her, but there are times she behaves strangely and argues too much. She says that I'm . . . " He hesitated. "The Ivanciches were very hospitable with us while we stayed in their home. I just want to return the favor." I prepared his bed, then went back to the kitchen and helped Fico prepare the next day's breakfast and lunch. Shortly, Mary walked into the pantry concerned, asking where he was. I told her he had gone to his room.

The following morning I went to his room. He was getting dressed. "Good morning, muchacho. I feel good this morning." I knew he had fallen asleep reading the night before. I had taken his glasses off and the book from his hands. I told him that Miss Mary had been very concerned about him, and he was pleasantly surprised. Whenever

Papa and Mary argued, Papa would wake up the next morning cheerful and serene, as if nothing had happened. She had learned to accept his radical behavior the same way she learned the art of in-house correspondence, as arguments were resolved via notes and letters left throughout the house for each other—a behavior much like that of dating adolescents.

After this blowup, Mary changed tactics. Instead of arguing with Hemingway and becoming bitter, she became the most understanding and sweetest wife a man could hope for. She graciously accompanied the Ivanciches around Havana and to different social events and provided the best comforts around the house. Her understanding and compliant attitude toward the guests infuriated Hemingway.

While things did get a little better between Mary and Papa, Hemingway still behaved like an awkward schoolboy whenever Adriana was around. He tried to be courteous and speak to Dora for a few minutes, but he always wound up concentrating his full attention on Adriana. When she wasn't speaking with him or swimming in the pool, Adriana spent time drawing and sketching in the library or flirting with numerous affluent young men from Havana who visited her at the Finca. On Sundays, she and Dora walked down to the pueblo and attended Mass at the little church built by the Franciscans in 1667 that was on a small hill not too far from the Finca. They had access to the car and Juan was at their disposal, but the women chose to make their Sunday pilgrimage on foot.

One afternoon Hemingway, Mary, and the Ivanciches were by the pool. Gianfranco swam laps around the pool and the others talked and basked in the sun. I brought ice and the cocktail mixer to prepare martinis.

Papa addressed me. "Miss Adriana sees your horse every morning grazing on the small hill. She would like to ride him. Can you borrow another horse from one of your brothers for Gianfranco?"

"It would be nice if they went out for a ride," Mary added with a gleam in her eyes.

"You should accompany them," Papa said to me. "They want to ride outside the Finca's grounds and we don't want them to get lost."

I looked at Adriana, and she gave me a coquettish smile. I smiled back. Dora caught my eye. I stopped smiling, excused myself, and went back to the house in a hurry.

The following day around noon, I arrived at the Finca on my horse with two horses in tow. I tied them in front of the garage and walked over to the bungalow. Adriana saw me, waved, and met me halfway.

"*Gianfranco non verrà,*" she said with a mischievous smile, "*buono.*" I told her that I didn't mind as long as her mother didn't object. She understood and laughed. She mounted my horse and I my brother's horse, Candela, a spirited stallion that was hard to handle. We rode out of the Finca and stopped by my house to leave the extra horse. Then we rode aimlessly. Adriana was a good rider and handled my horse with no problems. I was pleased that so far Trueno was behaving well. Adriana's beauty was overwhelming. I could see why Papa was mesmerized by her. I was too. She was beautiful, and a tremendous flirt. She knew exactly how to play a man and get his attention.

After we had been riding for a while, I noticed she was getting restless. In a playful gesture she rode past me and accidentally brushed my mount. Candela took that as a challenge and bucked on his hind legs and ran full spirited after her. The horse bit his brace and didn't allow me to steer. He was out of control. Adriana was a blur when I passed her. The wild horse ran close to the trees in an attempt to throw me off. I lost my balance and flew off the horse and hit a tree. I fell to the ground holding my chest in great pain, dazed and confused. Adriana caught up with me jumped off the horse and came to my side. Apologizing profusely, she kissed me several times. I kissed her back. An old farmer who lived nearby came over. He helped me up off the ground and talked us into going to his house to make sure I had no broken bones. "Este muchacho loco almost killed himself against a tree," el guajiro said to his wife when she came out of the house to see what the commotion was about.

Adriana held my one hand. I had my other hand on my chest. I was still bent over from the pain. Inside the small house we sat in the sparsely furnished living room.

"If you're hurting, you should drink some dirt water," the old woman said.

"No, I'll be alright," I said looking at Adriana, who was still holding my hand.

"Nonsense. I'll get some dirt water from the yard. It's good for the pain." The old woman motioned for us to follow. Adriana and I walked out into the backyard where there were goats and chickens. The old woman carried a tin cup in her hand. She bent over a puddle of water and scooped up some brown liquid. I looked at Adriana, who grimaced. We turned around and headed back to the living room to sit down.

The old woman followed us with the tin cup. "Here you go. Drink up," she insisted. I looked at Adriana, who held my hand tighter. We looked at the tin cup filled with the brown liquid.

"Rum. How about some rum?" interjected the old guajiro.

"Sí! Rum is better," I said smiling at him. Adriana's grip loosened. I took a shot of the rum, then another, and felt better. I wanted to buy the rum bottle from them, but they insisted that it was their gift to us. We took the bottle of rum and left the house. Adriana started to laugh and tapped the bottle with her nail, smiling. I winked at her, and she blushed.

We gathered the horses and headed to a nearby lake. She wanted to go swimming. When I told her that we didn't have swimwear with us, she smiled and took off her clothes down to her undergarments. She looked at me, raised an eyebrow, and smiled. I took off my clothes, and together jumped into the cool waters of the lake. We swam and held each other. She was beautiful, and her lips were sweet. She felt like heaven.

A couple of days later, late in the afternoon, I saw Hemingway by the terrace steps that lead to the pool. He called me over. I could see that he was very upset. I thought he had found out about Adriana and me. My heart pounded in my chest.

"We have a big problem," Hemingway said tensely. I was not going to volunteer any information.

I loved him like a father, and I knew how he felt about Adriana. But what happened between us just happened. I felt I had betrayed him. She liked his attention and flirted with him, but that was her nature. But I know she didn't care for him the way he wanted her to care.

"La señora Dora has lost her purse, with a great amount of money in it," Hemingway said, and I was relieved.

Dora and Adriana had gone to Havana with Juan in the morning, and after they returned to the Finca, Dora had lost the purse. The two new maids hired exclusively for the Ivanciches were trustworthy and had come highly recommended by Gregorio Fuentes.

"How about Fico?" Hemingway asked looking straight at me.

"Not Fico," I said, upset. Fico wouldn't do anything like that. He might have been mischievous when he was younger, but he wasn't a thief. Papa stared into my eyes and I held his stare. I thought that he was testing me to see if I broke down and confessed on Adriana.

"I've seen Fico in the mornings by the bungalow. He has no reason to be there!" Hemingway blurted. Fico helped Zoraida, one of the maids, with the breakfast trays, I told him. But it's not that he's such a gentleman. It was because he liked Zoraida. I said that it was an injustice to blame Fico, who probably had nothing to do with it. "You'll take his side!" Hemingway said getting more upset. I told him that I was not taking sides and that there was no proof. Hemingway insisted on blaming Fico for the disappearance of Dora's purse. He had focused his anger and blame on Fico and was prepared to fire him.

"It's an injustice! I resign! I can't work here any longer," I blurted out without much thought.

Hemingway didn't say anything and looked into my eyes again. He then turned around and went back to the house. I stood there for a couple of minutes and started to walk down to my house. As I walked away, I heard Mary calling out to me. I turned around and walked over to her.

"Don't go!" she pleaded with me. "You have to understand that Papa is not the same. He has been behaving very irrationally lately. This girl is driving him crazy," Mary admitted to me, and I knew it hurt her. "He's not thinking straight. You can't leave now. Not when we need you the most! I was going to leave him too, but I've stayed. We have to stick together. She'll be out of here soon and things will go back to normal." She looked at me, her blue eyes welling with tears.

"I'll stay," I said, and she gave me a faint smile. Mary said that Papa was very upset but knew that she would bring me back. "Papa didn't say a word when I resigned," I told her.

"You know he would not." She took hold of my arm and we walked up to the house. "The best thing is to act as if nothing has happened," she said with a smile and tear-glazed eyes.

The following morning Juan came in with a purse and a black silk scarf in hand, and immediately I went and got Hemingway. Juan explained exactly where he found the purse. Papa thanked him several times.

"Did you mention the disappearance of the purse to him yesterday?" Hemingway asked me after Juan went to the pantry.

"Not a word," I said, looking him in the eye.

Above: Raúl stands with his parents, Elpidia (Fanny) and René, in June of 2007 on the very same spot on the terrace at the Finca Vigía where they were photographed with Papa Hemingway in 1957.

Right: The Finca Vigía's majestic ceiba tree, ca. 1960s.

René with his sister, Nilda, on the Finca grounds in June of 2007.

Twin brothers René and Luis Villarreal stand in front of their childhood home at the foot of the gate to the Finca Vigía, 1996.

Martha Gellhorn photographed René in front of the Finca, ca. 1940.

The Villarreal boys and their friends playing baseball at the Finca Vigía, ca. 1940.

Hemingway sits on the terrace of the Finca, ca. 1939–40.

Fast friends Gigi (Gregory Hemingway), Popito (Rodolfo Villarreal), and Fico (Alberto Ramos) at the Finca Vigía, ca. 1940.

Above: Hemingway by the pool of the Finca Vigía, ca. 1939–40.

Right: A barefoot Hemingway at the Club de Cazadores in El Cerro before leaving in the spring of 1944 to report on the war.

Above: Hemingway with Gary Cooper and friends in a nightclub in Havana, ca. 1947–48. Winston Guest stands ar the far right.

Left: Papa and René watching a cockfight in a makeshift arena on the grounds of the Finca, ca. 1947–48. Photo by George Leavens.

Left: Chauffeur Juan López and René (seated) in Havana, ca. 1947.

Below, from left to right: Gregory Hemingway, Oscar Villarreal, Alberto Ramos (Fico), Juan López, Patrick Hemingway, and René Villarreal on the steps of the Capitolio Nacional in Havana, 1947.

Left: René, aka Kid Vigía, training as a boxer in 1949.

Below: Adriana Ivancich enjoying the cool waters of the Finca's pool in 1950.

Hemingway poses for photographs in his tower studio, ca. 1949–50.

Papa caught in a moment of relaxation, sitting in his favorite chair with Blackie (Black Dog) at his feet, ca. 1954. Photo by Roberto Herrera Sotolongo.

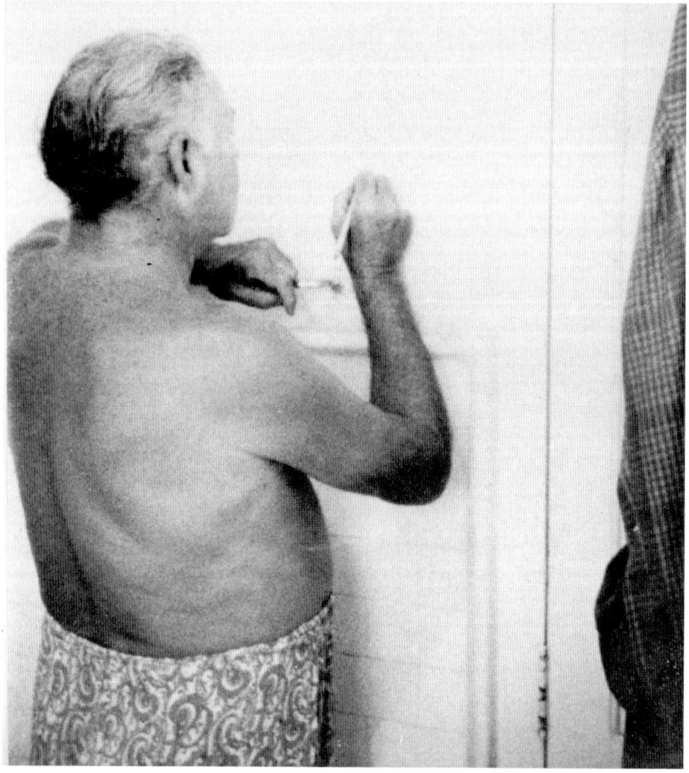

Above: As this 1954 photograph of Hemingway shows, he noted his weight on the bathroom wall every day. Photo by Earl Theisen.

Right: Papa, ca. 1955.

Papa reading in the shade by the pool, ca. 1955.

This 1955 photograph appeared in a *Look* magazine feature on Hemingway's Cuban life. Here, Earl Theisen caught the Hemingways dining with their "usual" guests. From left to right: Don Juan Duñabeita (Siskie/Simbad), Dr. José Luis Herrera Sotolongo, Hemingway, Mario (Mayito) Menocal Jr., Elicio Argüelles, and Mary. Photo by Earl Theisen.

Hemingway walking the grounds of the Finca Vigía in 1956. Photo by Hans Malmberg.

René introduced his fiancée, Elpidia (Fanny), to the Hemingways in March 1957. Fanny found Papa's attire interesting, unique. That morning he wore shorts, moccasins with no socks, and a sweater with a vest under it. Notice that Mary photographed them from the waist up.

Right: Hemingway with Blackie (Black Dog), ca. 1957. Photo by Roberto Herrera Sotolongo.

Below: Christmas 1957 at the Finca. Don Juan Duñabeita (Siskie/Simbad) stands in the background, the Richards sisters sit on either side of Mary, René kneels in the foreground, and Papa Hemingway is by Christmas tree.

A cheerful Papa stands by the typewriter in his workroom, ca. 1958. Photo by Ken Heyman.

René poses in Hemingway's study in 1964 when he was administrator and director of the Hemingway Museum.

René on the terrace of the Finca Vigía, 1996.

"Let's wait for Adriana and Dora to come after breakfast so they can look through it." Hemingway went to his room and waited for Adriana and Dora to come to the house.

The women were relieved that the purse had been found and that all the money was still there. Dora had withdrawn $27,000 from a bank in Havana for Gianfranco, who was planning to purchase a banana plantation. She had the purse with her yesterday morning, and after returning to the Finca with several bags from the Havana stores, she had placed the purse and scarf down with the bags somewhere by the garage. She forgot the purse when she picked up the bags and went to the bungalow.

Hemingway was relieved that the purse had been recovered and there had been no foul play. Juan didn't even know what was inside the purse. I'm sure if he had known he still would have returned it. Papa never mentioned the altercation we had, and I never brought it up. Fico remained oblivious to the entire incident. I never told him he had been the accused. He would have been hurt.

For the next few months, late at night, after everyone had gone to bed, Adriana and I rendezvoused by the pool. We stayed out until the early-morning hours, when we would quietly make our way back to our rooms. I don't know if Hemingway knew, or if anyone else did. But I suspect Gianfranco was aware that something was going on.

In February of 1951, Dora and Adriana were preparing to return to Venice. Gianfranco was to stay behind in Cuba and look after his newly acquired banana plantation. Hemingway and Mary planned a large farewell party for their departing guests. They hired serving staff for the grand event and rented tables and chairs from El Floridita. It was the biggest party ever at the Finca. Adriana's gentlemen callers appeared in their starched shirts and expensive suits. She had a long line of suitors waiting for the opportunity to dance with her. Hemingway seemed upset by the younger and more elegant competition.

During the party, I mostly took care of Papa and Mary and made sure the extra help had all they needed. Once in a while I caught Adriana's eye while she danced. She would faintly smile back to me over the shoulder of one of her admirers. Throughout that night I hurt as I watched her in the arms of other men. There was nothing I could do. We were from different times, places, races, and social strata. When she left, she gave me the address of her family estate in Venice and said that if I ever found my way in Venice I was to look her up. She sent me several postcards from Europe, and I wrote a few letters to her. But after a couple of years it all stopped. And as years passed, the beautiful, exotic, sultry Adriana became merely an enduring memory of a young, illicit love.

A couple of months after his mother and sister had returned to Venice, Gianfranco was still at the Finca, though planning to move closer to the plantation he had purchased. One afternoon on the way back to the Finca with the mail, I stopped at my house. My mother was very upset and told me that Gianfranco had to take Fico to the hospital. Fico had shot himself, she said, and Clara, Mary's maid, had stayed to mind the house. (Papa and Mary were on a fishing trip.)

I rushed up to the Finca and found Clara nervously sitting in the pantry. She explained that she had been cleaning Mary's room and that Gianfranco was in his room when they both heard the shot. They ran to the living room and found Fico pale as a ghost holding the smoking rifle in his hand and bleeding from the shoulder. Clara had cleaned the bloodstain from the floor and showed me where the bullet exited and had lodged in the molding of the front door. The .22 caliber bullet had made only a small entry hole but had destroyed the molding when it exited. I called Pancho and had him fix the door.

When I heard Gianfranco's car approach, I went to meet them. I saw Gianfranco alone and feared the worst. He told me to calm down, that Fico was alright but too embarrassed to come up so he had stayed at my house. I waited for Fico the rest of the afternoon and then finally decided to go down to my house to see if he was still there. He was gone. He told my mother that he was not going back to the Finca ever again. Fico's shame and embarrassment were not only because he accidentally shot himself; it was also because Zoraida had refused his love for her.

In the fall of 1952, *Life* magazine published the complete text of *The Old Man and the Sea*. I remember when Hemingway started working on the book earlier in 1951. Mary had reacted very favorably after she read the first draft, commenting that it was magnificent. *Across the River and into the Trees* had received overwhelmingly negative press, and many critics thought that Hemingway was finished as a writer. Papa commented how "they" circled him like sharks smelling blood. After ten years without publishing a book, he immersed himself in writing what he thought was his best work to date. Hemingway felt that he needed to redeem himself. He wanted a rematch, he told me, as much as a former boxing champion wants to regain his crown. He put a lot of pressure on himself to produce something spectacular. He was concerned with his long-term financial situation as well as his reputation as a writer. He told me that now, when he was older and had fought hard all his life to achieve fame and wealth, he should be able to enjoy life but couldn't do so. He said that if he ever needed money, no one would purchase his old Finca filled with so many old books, and fame was something one could not sell.

Perhaps driven by the same desire as Santiago, the old fisherman in *The Old Man and the Sea,* Papa didn't let himself be defeated or destroyed. I believe that he pulled the story of the old Cuban fisherman from the extensive land, air, and sea war manuscript that he had been working on off and on for a number of years, the manuscript he often referred to during his writing dry spells. I remember how diligently he worked revising the story of the old man.

It was around this time that the incident with Big Goats and the chameleon took place. Papa rushed out of his room one day, pencil in hand. "Come quick!" he called excitedly and went to the terrace. "Big Goats is fighting with a large chameleon." The cat was playing with his prey, biting and clawing it. And though the lizard fought back with unquestionable courage, it was no match for the large cat. Papa tried to save the chameleon, but it died. "He was destroyed and wouldn't allow himself to be defeated," Papa said. It was then that he placed the courageous chameleon in his bathroom as a reminder of the noble spirit.

The early reviews and reactions to *The Old Man and the Sea* were positive, and during that time Hemingway appeared to be happy and in top form. Whenever he read a favorable review, he would shadowbox, jabbing with the left, following with a straight right, and finishing with a left hook—con la izquierda y fácil (with the left and easy).

I was very curious about the story of the old man. I knew that he had been inspired by several old Cuban fishermen he had met in Cojímar. Papa had listened to their stories with great interest. However, I had to wait until it was published in Spanish. When I read it, I was impressed by the direct and simple prose and the wonderful story of the noble old fisherman who dreamed of lions on the beach. And I was very proud of what Papa had written about Cuba and its people.

THE MEN IN WHITE COATS

By 1953, I had been working as the Hemingways' majordomo for almost seven years and had the daily routines down to a science. Usually around 11:00 A.M. we received the ice delivery. Each morning when I heard the truck drive up to the house, I rushed to the pantry and made room for the ice in the refrigerator. Then I went out and shooed away the cats and dogs sleeping on the kitchen stairs. The driver then came up the steps and into the pantry and left the block of ice for me to break.

One morning a younger deliveryman came to the house. He was covering for the regular man, who was sick. The man carried the large block of ice up the steps to the kitchen. Ramón held the door open for him. As the young man reached the last step, he lost his footing and fell backward, down all twelve steps. The massive ice block hit the second step and broke in half. The frightened young man quickly got to his feet. Ramón and I rushed down to his aide. We saw traces of blood and asked him if he was hurt. He assured us he had not been injured but feared that one of the cats or dogs may have been hit by the block of ice. Hemingway had heard the noise from his workroom and walked over to the dining room. I explained to him what had happened and that we thought that one of the cats or dogs may be injured. Concerned, Papa rushed and met me by the kitchen steps.

The deliveryman apologized profusely and left in a hurry. Mary came down from the tower with Pancho, where they had been measuring and discussing the design of more furniture for the third floor. We followed the trail of blood hoping to find the poor animal that had been injured. I found Wiwi in the bushes not far from the steps. The cat had been crushed by the block of ice and was losing a lot of blood. "It looks really bad," Hemingway said, examining the cat. His face was flushed and his eyes watered. He sat next to the cat and began to caress its head.

I phoned our veterinarian, Dr. Lagarde, who told me there was nothing he could do and that Hemingway knew exactly what had to be done. Papa was still caressing the cat when I got back to him. "I know what I have to do. Bring me the .22 caliber rifle," he said in a low voice, tears rolling down his cheeks. I came back with the rifle. Softly, Papa caressed and spoke to Wiwi. He looked at me. I helped him stand up. He composed himself. I handed him the rifle. His eyes welled with tears. I could see the hesitation in his face. I started to cry.

"Papa, do you want me to do it?" I asked.

"No, I must do it. It's my duty." Hemingway looked at Wiwi and more tears came down his face. "Call out to him. Stand in front of him and call out to him. I don't want him to see me shoot."

Papa walked behind Wiwi and put the end of the rifle behind the cat's head. He hesitated, looked at me. I locked my eyes on him. He looked down. *Bang!* Not looking at my face, he handed me the rifle, weeping as I had never seen him do before. "Take care of the rest," he said before he rushed up to the house.

I waited for Papa to reach the house, then followed him in. He went to his bathroom. I locked the rifle back in the closet of his study and then went to the living room to find an old copy of the *New York Times* to wrap Wiwi in. As I cleaned the blood from the steps, I heard Papa loudly arguing in the living room. I ran to the kitchen, where Ramón waited for me.

"Hurry, hurry, caballero is very angry!" Ramón said as he held the door open for me. By the time I got to the living room, Hemingway had gone into his workroom.

Mary rushed to me crying, asking where the rifle was. I told her it was locked in the studio. "It's good that you locked the rifle. If not Papa would have shot those two men." The men she spoke of had ignored the signs by the gate deterring unwanted or unannounced visitors and driven up to the house. They had let themselves in, and Mary had surprised them in the living room. They told her that they were from the States and worked in a clinic for the mentally deranged. They had come to Cuba on vacation and simply wanted to visit Hemingway.

Papa was distraught when he entered the house after shooting Wiwi, and finding the intruders in the living room made him even more upset. One of the men made a cruel comment regarding Hemingway crying over having to shoot one of his cats. I never saw the men. I think that if Papa had had the rifle he would have shot them both.

About an hour later Mary convinced Papa to go to the pool. I went to the kitchen to prepare drinks and wondered what kind of people would enter a home without being invited or announced and try to carry on a conversation with someone who is obviously very upset. I took the drinks to them by the pool. Papa seemed calmer, reading the newspapers. When I carried out the second round of drinks, I took along the small Zenith portable radio and placed it on a small table next to him and tuned it to the classical station.

"Remember when I brought Wiwi back from Cojímar. A fisherman from Guanabacoa had given him to me," Papa said looking up from the newspaper.

"Yes, he was very playful then. And if we had not gotten wise, he would have finished off our pigeons."

"But lately he wasn't as good a hunter as he used to be," Papa said, taking a sip from his drink. "He was too old and too fat to be a successful hunter. But he still tried." I agreed. "When he was younger he was really good. Really good."

AFRICAN SAFARI

In 1953 we suffered a great lost at the Finca when Ramón Wong died from a heart attack.

One day after lunch Ramón started to feel very ill, so Juan and I drove him to Calixto Garcia Hospital in Havana. I sat in the backseat of the stationwagon with him. He was gasping for air and coming in and out of consciousness. "Apurate Juan. Apurate!" I yelled to Juan. Ramón's eyes rolled back in his head and he held tight to my hand. His breathing became more desperate. Then his body relaxed in my arms.

Ramón's wife was contacted and the funeral arrangements made. Papa wanted to cover the funeral expenses and provide financial assistance for the children's education, but his widow declined any financial help. We found out that Ramón had been a shrewd businessman. Not only did he have a good insurance policy, but he belonged to an organization that would take care of his wife and kids. He also had a partnership in a restaurant in Havana's Chinatown.

Unfortunately, his replacement turned out to be a drunk. Once a great master chef, Agustin Antuña, a Basque, had drunk his way out of great jobs and fine establishments. In the four days he was at the Finca, he severely depleted the liquor inventory. "This man must be very rich," Agustin said to me the afternoon I found him sitting in the pantry room next to two empty bottles of Château Margaux. I confronted him and he responded with a devil-may-care attitude. Hemingway fired Agustin within a couple of days, and Mary took on the cooking responsibilities for a while.

Some months later we suffered another tragedy. Clara, Mary's maid, suffered from bouts with depression. One evening when she was severely depressed, she stopped and briefly spoke to my mother, telling her that she was bored with life. She then went to see her family and Arturito, her son, in the town of Casa Blanca in Havana. Early the next morning, a neighbor banged on my parents' door and informed them that Clara had been found unconscious behind the pueblo's bakery and had been rushed to the clinic. She had taken a whole bottle of sleeping pills and was in a coma. She died a short while later.

Hemingway and Mary planned an East African safari for mid-1953. Papa had not been to Africa since 1934. They were to be away for several months. Before ending up in East Africa, they would travel to New York, London, France, Italy, and Spain. After fifteen years of vowing not to step onto Spanish soil until the last of his friends from the civil war was released, Hemingway was going back to Spain. He wanted to reestablish old connections in the bullfighting world.

That spring an editor for *Look* magazine traveled to Cuba and tried to persuade Hemingway to allow a photographer to accompany Papa and Mary on the safari. The magazine wanted a picture story of 3,500 words or more and Hemingway to write the photo captions. The proposed payment was an offer Hemingway didn't refuse.

Hemingway invited Cuban boxer Evelio Mustelier, alias Kid Tunero, Cuba's former middleweight champion, and his family to stay at the Finca while he and Mary were away. He was one of Hemingway's heroes, and also one of mine. Hemingway wrote an article on Kid Tunero for *La Prensa Libre,* a Havana newspaper, in which he declared him to be one of the last true gentlemen in and out of the ring. Papa and I had seen Kid Tunero's last fight, when he fought as a light heavyweight against Hanskin Barrow. During his career, Kid Tunero was known as "the gentleman of the ring" because of his classic style and quiet demeanor. Later in his career he was also known as "the champion without a crown" for defeating two world middleweight champions. Those fights had not been for the crown, however, and Kid Tunero never received his much-deserved world title.

After Evelio, Yolette, and their two sons moved into the house, I learned that Kid Tunero and Luis Sarria, another great Cuban boxer (who in later years became a respected trainer and masseur for Muhammad Ali), were training fighters at the Rafael Conde gymnasium in Lauto, Havana. With Mary and Papa away, I had more free time and asked if I could join the gym and train as a boxer. Tunero told me that it was a brutal sport and unless I was an extraordinary fighter, I could easily end up broken, poor, and in bad health.

Despite his warning, after a couple months of training I started a boxing career as a welterweight. I fought under my old alias, Kid Vigía. After winning five fights—three by knockout, two by decision—and losing one, I ended my short professional boxing career. I enjoyed the sport but lacked the discipline needed to become a true champion. At twenty-four I was really more interested in riding horses and pursuing women. But even after my last fight, I kept on training. I didn't want to lose touch with the sport.

I received many letters from the Hemingways telling me about where they had visited and whom they had seen. Papa wrote me about the bullfighting world in Spain, and Mary wrote telling me of the black-maned lion she had shot in Africa. It was clear that they were having a good time. Both Papa and Mary sounded happy in their letters.

Then, on January 23, 1954, the Finca received a telephone call from a news station asking for more information on the Hemingways' fatal plane crash in Africa. Tunero answered the call and told the reporter he knew nothing about the crash. For the second time Ernest Hemingway was reported dead in the world press. Again, deep down in my being, I knew he was still alive. It was the very same feeling I had had when I was just a child and heard that he'd been killed in a car accident in London.

Anxiously, we all waited for more news. Finally good news came: confirmation from the radio that they were safe and unharmed. But within just a day, we learned of a second plane crash. This time Papa suffered serious injuries to his head and back. To escape the burning plane, he had used his head as a battering ram to butt the door open. He had suffered another concussion. Mary, already aching from the first accident, further damaged her knee and had numerous scratches. From Nairobi they went straight away to Venice, where Papa began a slow recovery.

Mayito Menocal, whom Papa had invited to accompany them on the safari, had returned to Cuba as soon as the safari had ended. He wanted to reciprocate Papa's generosity in covering his expenses on the safari, so he asked me what I thought el viejo would like as a gift. I told him that Papa had pretty much everything he wanted. Mayito decided that his gift to Papa would be to pave the gravel road from the gate to the house. Mayito, Elicio Argüelles, and other Spanish-speaking friends of Papa referred to him as el viejo—but never in front of him, only in his absence. "El viejo" is also used as a term of endearment for an old friend or father. They asked me to never tell Papa that they referred to him that way.

By May of 1954, Papa had recovered and was ready to travel again. From Venice he wanted to go to Spain for the San Isidro Feast to see Luis Miguel Dominguín and Antonio Ordóñez, the two great matadors of the era. There he was also attended by his old doctor, Juan Manuel Madinaveitia, who put him on a strict diet. From Spain, he and Mary returned to Venice before boarding the *Francesco Morosini* at Genoa.

After fifteen months away, they were clearly very happy to be back home. The mountains of trunks and luggage and boxes contained animal heads and other exotic trophies from Africa—walking sticks, figurines, and even a camel saddle. As souvenirs, Papa gave me an oryx head and a Masai lance.

He asked, "What are you going to do with them?"

"I'm going to show them to my family and my girlfriend. She is meeting my parents tonight," I said, smiling.

"She must be something special for you to introduce her to your parents."

"Her name is Elpidia, but everyone calls her Fanny. She and her family moved here from Santa Clara."

Hemingway looked at me, surprised. "It seems you're very happy. I look forward meeting her. I'll tell Miss Mary the good news."

It was great to have Papa and Mary back. I felt that this was a new era for us at the Finca.

THE NOBEL PRIZE

After the second plane crash in Africa, Hemingway suffered chronic back pain. I often gave him back massages using the lion lard he had brought back from safari. It seemed to ease the pain somewhat, but I was no masseur. Lily, the manicurist, told us that Frankie Steinhart hired a masseur three times a week. Mary, who had a much better relationship with the Steinharts, looked into the matter and was able to get the man to come over and massage Papa.

It turned out that the masseur was Mario "Kid" Sánchez, a one-time national boxing champion in the featherweight division. He was nervous, fast-talking, and entertained us with his anecdotes of the ring. In no time he won Papa's affection. Papa often told me that Mario was punch-drunk but a joy to have around. It wasn't long before Mario was coming to the Finca five days a week.

Mary oversaw the strict, low-sodium diet the Spanish doctor had prescribed for Hemingway. She also saw to it that he significantly reduce his consumption of alcohol and get plenty of rest. She insisted that Papa have only one whiskey shot a day and no more than three glasses of wine.

Spanish matador Luis Miguel Dominguín visited the Finca for a couple of weeks in August of 1954. Hemingway and Mary took him fishing on the *Pilar* and showed him around Havana. On several occasions Papa and I took him to the cockfights in El Cotorro. He also showed the bullfighter several of the lances he had brought back from Africa and demonstrated their use during a lion hunt. Numerous young ladies from the pueblo asked permission to come up and get his autograph, and the handsome Spaniard gladly obliged. During his stay in Cuba, Dominguín expressed his curiosity about Afro-Cuban religious practices. Perhaps the matador wanted to find out about his fate in the bullring. Juan drove him to Guanabacoa, a town a few miles north of San Francisco de Paula known for its powerful and wise Babalaos, high priests in the Order of Ocha, a religion that combines Catholic and Yoruba beliefs (widely known as Santería).

A couple of weeks after Luis Miguel Dominguín left the Finca, the beautiful American movie star Ava Gardner came to visit for a couple of days and to rest and enjoy the Cuban sun. (Hemingway believed she had fallen in love with the young matador in Spain and had followed him to Cuba.) The local press announced her stay in the Vigía, and the presence of this famous beauty caused an uproar among the young men of San Francisco de Paula.

One morning as I came up from the pueblo with the mail, I saw a group of young boys jumping the fence and making their way up to the house. I followed them from afar. When they got close to the pool, they hid behind trees. Ah! I could see what had boldened the young men to take such intrusive actions. Ava Gardner was swimming nude in the cool waters of the pool. I walked up to them and asked what they were up to. They said they wanted her autograph. I told them it would be better if they left and came up later to ask permission, just as the young ladies had done when Luis Miguel Dominguín had visited. They agreed and left quietly.

I couldn't blame them. She was a beautiful woman indeed. I watched Miss Gardner swim for a few minutes, before taking a deep breath and going inside to give Papa the mail. I told him what was going on outside. To avoid any further problems, he suggested to Miss Gardner that she sunbathe on the roof of the tower, where no one could see her, and that she skinny-dip only when they were out in the *Pilar*. I had a strange feeling I had just shot myself in the foot.

During the brief time Ava Gardner was at the Finca, she managed to have every male guest on his knees. I remember a lunch party Papa and Mary gave in her honor. Mayito Menocal was invited, as was his son Mayitin and Gianfranco Ivancich and Siskie. She flirted with all of them. Mary watched in amusement as the men fought for Ava's attention. She was very glad that Papa was not one of them. Miss Gardner left her other gentlemen callers behind and hitched a ride to Havana with Gianfranco in his old, rusty, beat-up Volkswagen. On the way to Havana she took off her expensive shoes and dropped them in the back seat of the car, which had holes on the floor. They had to stop at a store in Havana, where Gianfranco bought her 25-cent espadrilles before dropping her off at the Floridita.

By 1954 Papa had already received the Pulitzer Prize as well as another major literary prize from Italy. Late that October, it was rumored that Ernest Hemingway would be awarded the Nobel Prize for literature. Phone calls and well-wishes came from all over the world. The small pueblo post office was inundated with mail and telegrams.

Papa appeared to be calm, but I knew he was nervous and anxious. He insisted on diligently working as usual until the official word came. He was working on his safari book. One morning when I served him breakfast, he asked, "René, you know when I write best?" He was standing in front of the typewriter. "Morning, early in the morning is when I do my best work. The mind is clear and sharp from a good night's rest. It's even better if what you write is yours, your own personal experiences. That's when it all works. It doesn't matter what length of time has passed if the memory still lives. You can write it down with ease. The details you fill in afterwards."

The Nobel Prize announcement came on October 28, 1954, and the celebrations began. "It's official," Papa said, embracing Mary. "Put some champagne on ice." He looked at me, smiling.

"Already done. I'll go get it." I had iced some bottles when the rumors began swirling days earlier. "Congratulations Papa," I said, extending my hand. He shook my hand and we hugged. He hugged me hard. He was so happy. I was as proud as a son could be of his father.

Over the next few days the phone didn't stop ringing. The poor old mailman made numerous trips to the Finca with telegrams. (Hemingway gave him a generous tip each time.) And there were countless congratulatory telephone calls and visits from friends. Hemingway suggested that I get an assistant to run errands and fetch the mail from the pueblo. He told me there would be many more visitors coming soon. I hired Pedrito, a 15-year-old friend of mine who was looking for a job at the time. He was a hard worker and trustworthy. Mary and Papa liked him immediately.

Papa disliked public speaking to the point that it kept him from traveling to Stockholm in December to accept his Nobel Prize in person. Instead he sent an acceptance speech that was read to the Swedish

Academy by the U.S. ambassador to Sweden. Papa pardoned his absence with the excuse that he was still recovering from the injuries he suffered from the African crashes. I knew this to be true. Though Papa tried to downplay it, his injuries had changed him. He was not the same man who had left for Africa in 1953. His aura of invincibility had disappeared, and for the first time in my eyes he appeared frail.

The people of the pueblo greatly respected Hemingway and took great pride in his accomplishments. This small, poor town of San Francisco de Paula was home to a man who brought the Nobel Prize to its humble gates, and the people of the pueblo also paid their respects. After the announcement, a group had come up to the terrace to congratulate him. Papa greeted them with a great smile and in careful Spanish told them he was thankful for their attention and jubilee. He said he would always be there with them. He greeted each and every one of them while I served each a shot of rum. We then toasted to the Nobel Prize and to Mr. Way.

San Francisco de Paula had always been a poor town with very few employment opportunities. Unless you were lucky enough to own a business, the only chances for jobs were in a factory that canned guava and coconut, the large stone quarry, or at the Hatuey beer distillery in El Cotorro. The people of San Francisco de Paula were honest, modest, and simple.

For years, we only had one policeman patrolling the streets. One night a group of us drank in one of the local bars, and Pedro Herrera, the lone policeman, joined us. After a few drinks he confessed that his gun holster was filled with nothing more than old newspapers. In all the years he had patrolled the streets, he had not carried a gun. In town everyone knew each other, and he knew that if there was ever a crime, the town would assist in the capture of the criminal.

We heard rumors that the Carretera Central highway was to be improved. This would mean more employment possibilities for the pueblo. The road was to be widened, which meant that the small wooden houses along the side of the road would be demolished. The owners of the old houses received compensation and had the opportunity to build new homes somewhere else. But there was also disturbing news, that the town of Guanabacoa planned to run pipes from its aqueduct through our town and not let us take advantage of the water supply. During the dry season, San Francisco de Paula at times went a couple of days without water. (The year before it had gotten so bad that Hemingway had the ill-fated well reopened and allowed the people of the town to enter the Finca and get water.) The town met and tried to raise money to bribe the contractors to have a line from the aqueduct's water supply for San Francisco de Paula. But when the pueblo came up short of money to pay the contractors, they asked me to speak with Hemingway on their behalf. I did so, and Hemingway wrote a check for the sum needed to bribe the contractors.

On July 21, 1954, the same day he celebrated his 55th birthday, he had received the highest Cuban civilian award: the decoration from the Order of Carlos Manuel de Céspedes. And in August 1955, the owner of the Hatuey beer brewery in El Cotorro wanted to honor Hemingway by giving him a brand new yacht. The man wanted to thank Hemingway for all the free advertising he had received by mentioning Hatuey beer in *The Old Man and the Sea*. Papa declined, however, and said that he would rather have the brewery host a dinner party in his honor and invite his friends from San Francisco de Paula, fishermen from Cojímar, and others from surrounding villages. For that wonderful event, the Hatuey brewery produced a thousand beer mugs with a drawing of Hemingway and a poem printed on them.

El amigo Hemingway
goza, pesca, y escribe
y mejor la vida vive
tomando cerveza Hatuey

Our friend Hemingway
Enjoys, fishes, and writes
and better lives life
drinking Hatuey Beer

THE CEIBA TREE

Mary kept herself busy making sure that the Finca looked its best for the endless stream of visitors and guests. In her scrutiny of the house, she came across the damaged floor tiles in the living room, dining room, and Papa's workroom. The roots of the large ceiba tree out front had been pushing up the floor tiles for years, but there was no way anyone could convince Papa to chop down the ceiba in order to restore the tiles. I had simply placed the kudu skin rug over the damaged tiles in his room and the matting over the damage in the living room. But the dining room was harder to conceal.

Mary secretly planned to restore the tiles in the dining room. After weeks spent planning, and after finding the same exact Spanish mamey-colored tiles in a Havana shop, she faked illness early one morning and begged off of a scheduled fishing trip. As soon as Papa left, driven by Juan, Mary called in the workers and the job was started. Everything went according to plan and schedule. The workers performed as expected. They took no breaks and worked as fast as possible. The piece of root was chopped off, the dirt removed, and the tiles replaced.

But just as the workers were finishing, Mary heard a car pull up the driveway and saw Juan opening the door of the Chrysler for Papa. She hurried back to the dining room and told the workers to clean up and rushed them out the back door of the kitchen. In their rush, the men left a small shovel leaning against the wall. Hemingway walked to the living room, then to the dining room, where Mary greeted him. The fishing trip had been cut short due to bad weather, he said. Hemingway then saw the shovel leaning against the wall and the white dust around the tiles. In seconds he pieced everything together. He turned red with rage.

"Who cut the root?! I always told you no, NO, NO!! Who cut the root?!" he asked several times. Mary froze. He demanded again for her to tell him. Mary told him it was someone from the pueblo whom she had contracted. Hemingway picked up the shovel, opened one of the windows of the dining room, and hurled it out. He went over to his workroom and began to pace around the room like a caged lion. When he returned to the dining room, Mary was not there. He then went to her room and began to argue with her again. She cried and only half-heartedly argued back. She came out of her room and told me she was going to the pool to give him time to cool off. He then came out and approached me.

"Did you know anything about this?" he demanded. In his eyes I could see disappointment that I had taken part in the conspiracy.

"Yes," I said.

"Why didn't you tell me?"

"You've told me that when you're not here, Miss Mary runs the house. When you both are out, I run the house. Today she was here," I said, offering my only defense. He didn't say anything and just looked at me understanding that I had not taken sides. Telling on Mary would have been cowardly, and I would have lost her trust forever. He knew that was not my style.

He then asked me to find the piece of the chopped-off root and bring it back to the house. "It belongs here in the house!" I found the piece of root, cleaned it, and leaned it against a wall of the dining room. He walked back from his room and looked at the piece of root. His face grew stormy again.

"Where's Miss Mary?"

"She said she was going down to the pool."

"Please make me a gin and tonic. I'll be in the living room. I won't go down until she comes up. I don't want to start arguing again."

I went to prepare the drink, but when I got back he wasn't there. I went to his workroom and bathroom and still didn't find him. I looked out to the terrace and saw him by the cistern contemplating the large ceiba tree. I opened the door and went out to the terrace.

"You think it'll damage the ceiba?" Hemingway asked without taking his eyes off the massive tree.

"No, I don't think so. Had it been a main root, perhaps."

I gave him the drink. He took a long sip and looked at the tree again. "Drink is a bit weak," he said holding the glass up, then looking at me.

"The roots of the ceiba probably extend beyond the house. I don't think that small piece of root will damage it," I said, ignoring his comment on the drink.

"You're right. I don't think it will hurt the ceiba." He took another sip.

Papa waited for Mary to finish her swim and come back up to the house, before gathering a few books and magazines and going to the pool. By the time I got there with the radio, he was already in the water swimming (nude, as was his custom). I turned on the radio to his favorite classical station.

"Gracias, muchacho," he said as I was about to leave. "When you come down again, bring the cocktail mixer and plenty of ice. It's time we break this strict diet. I'm going to forget all this nonsense. I won't have lunch with Miss Mary. As far as she's concerned, I'm still out fishing. Tell her I'm eating alone and not to throw away the root in the dining room. Tell her I say it is where it belongs. You can make me a peanut butter sandwich with lots of white onions. And bring a bottle of chianti."

I did not like how Papa used the incident of the ceiba root as an excuse to completely abandon his diet. I found Mary sitting in the living room and, concerned for his well-being, explained what had gone on.

"This is horrible. He's only hurting himself," she said upset. "I guess, he asked you to find the piece of root and bring it back to the house."

"It's in the dining room, leaning against a wall."

"Don't you see! You know he only wants it there to start arguments whenever he sees it."

"He told me he didn't want to argue anymore. He just wanted to be alone."

"Yes, alone to break his diet and do as he pleases! He told me to leave him. I almost did. I love him a great deal, and I will not leave and let him destroy himself! This was all my fault. I should have never disobeyed him," she cried. Trying to console her, I told her that he'd be fine in a couple of days.

Days passed and there was still no communication between them. Papa ate and slept in his workroom. The only time they dined together was when there were guests and appearances had to be kept up. He refused to eat breakfast and insisted on his morning "juice" instead. He no longer even tried to conceal the popping noise of the cork. Mary grew very concerned when she realized he wasn't having breakfast, was eating very little for lunch and dinner, and was drinking heavily. She pleaded with me to persuade him to eat. I told her I would try my best. Boise, his favorite cat, wasn't eating either. He missed Hemingway feeding him breakfast in the mornings.

After almost a week of this behavior, I went in his room. He was by the typewriter, frowning. I bid him good morning.

"You look worried," he said.

"I have a big problem," I said seriously.

"What's wrong? How can I help?" Hemingway walked over to me. "Que pasa, muchacho. Tell me!" He put his hand on my shoulder.

"I'm in trouble. I'm in trouble with Boise, Miss Mary, and you."

"What do you mean Boise, Miss Mary, and me?"

I explained that he refused to have breakfast and that Miss Mary insisted I talk him into eating something in the morning. "She's also worried because you have abandoned the doctor's diet. And Boise won't eat because he wants you to feed him." I gave him a slight smile.

Hemingway looked at me. Boise came into the room and jumped on the bed. Papa walked over to the bed. "You hungry boy? You want something to eat?" He stroked the cat from head to tail. The cat stretched and met his hand with its head whenever he was stroked. "Let's solve some of the problems right now. Take that bottle of vodka and put it back in the living room where it belongs. I'll have breakfast this morning. I want *grapefruit* juice. Don't forget Boise's portion. He looks hungry." I nodded and went to the kitchen and picked up the tray with the already-prepared breakfast.

In October of 1955, we were getting ready for the hurricane season. Since coming to work at the Finca, we had spent the last months of the year preparing for a hurricane. We made sure we had lanterns, batteries for the portable radio, extra food, and bottled water.

On one of those stormy afternoons, we lost the electrical power in the house. I was able to get Raúl Portela, the electrician, to the Finca that same evening. I went out into the pouring rain to meet him by the gate. He came with an eager and young new assistant. I got in their truck and we drove up to the main electrical post in front of the house.

While Portela and I went to see where the problem originated,

Manolo, the assistant, geared up and went to the back of the house and found that the electricity cables were tangled with the branches of a güira tree. He climbed the tree and proceeded to cut the branches with his machete.

Portela and I were still in the front of the house when we heard the screams coming from one of the windows of Mary's room. "Stop what you're doing! Stop and drop the machete immediately! It's forbidden to cut any tree in this Finca! Who gave you permission?!" Hemingway was screaming furiously out of the window.

Portela and I realized what had happened and ran to the back of the house. By the time we got there, Hemingway was already outside and shaking the massive trunk of the tree, demanding that Manolo come down and face him like a man. Terrified, Manolo held on for dear life as the tree rocked back and forth. Hemingway stopped shaking the tree and picked up a large piece of branch that Manolo had chopped off. Portela told Mary and me to distract Hemingway in order to give him a chance to get Manolo down from the tree. Mary called Papa over to give him a raincoat, but he refused it. Portela seized the opportunity, stood under the tree, and yelled at Manolo to come down, saying that he was fired for disobeying his orders. Manolo came down the tree, ran to the front of the house, and jumped in the truck.

Hemingway approached Portela, who immediately asked to be excused for his assistant's behavior. I went to the front of the house to check on poor Manolo. I told him not to worry, that his boss was going to fix things up with Hemingway. Manolo told me of his incredibly bad luck. It wasn't enough that in his first week in a new job he was attacked by a pack of dogs, but today he infuriates un americano loco who wanted to kill him with the branch of a tree! And now, to top it all off, he gets fired for doing his job—all on the same day his wife tells him she is pregnant.

I told him not to move from the truck and went to the back of the house. Portela had been working on the cables and in a few minutes restored the electric power.

Portela said he had neglected to mention to his young apprentice not to use the machete on any tree in the Finca. I said that I thought it was a shame for the young man to lose his job just when he needed it the most. I explained that his wife was expecting their first child. Hemingway, who held the large piece of branch in his hand, followed our conversation. He told Portela not to fire the young man. It had been just a simple problem of poor communication. Papa said he was going to change into dry clothes and asked Portela to come up to the kitchen for a hot cup of coffee or a strong drink to warm up. He also asked me to invite Manolo to come in. I went out to the front of the house but could not convince Manolo to leave the truck. I went back to the kitchen and prepared café for everyone.

Later, Papa called me to the pantry and handed me two envelopes with checks inside. He told me to give them to Portela and Manolo. "Make sure Portela tells all his assistants not to use a machete when they come to work here. Give them some fish from the freezer and thank them on my behalf for responding so quickly."

The following morning when I served Hemingway his breakfast, I saw the güira tree branch leaning against one of the walls in his workroom. With his pocket knife, Papa had trimmed and rounded the ends and made it into a walking stick.

"What do you think of my new walking stick?" he asked. "I plan to use it when I go out for my walks. It has been difficult walking with Blackie lately. The neighbors have dogs, and the cars on the street also bother him. I think it is safer for him to stay here at home."

For some time Papa had enjoyed long walks around the Finca grounds with Blackie (Black Dog) by his side. But not long before this, Blackie had been attacked by one of Frankie Steinhart's large dogs. Papa had tried to get between the dogs and in the scuffle was scratched on the forearm. I was in the living room when Hemingway had returned. Very upset, he explained what had happened and how he had called out for the Steinharts to help him but no one came. Infuriated, he asked for his .22 caliber rifle. Together we walked over to the Steinharts' property line. Papa yelled for Frankie to come out and face him. We saw someone move behind the curtains from one of the windows of the house, but no one appeared. Instead, the large dog responded to the challenge and charged at us. "Puta madre!" Hemingway fired three shots in the air. The dog stopped in his tracks, turned, and ran, disappearing around the Steinharts' house. Hemingway handed me the rifle and we calmly walked back to the Finca.

Later, on the afternoons Papa took his walks around the pueblo without Blackie and with his new walking stick, I saw him at times pick up small rocks and bat them as if he was playing baseball.

IN THE LION'S DEN

After winning the Nobel Prize, and with the incredible success of *The Old Man and the Sea,* Hemingway seemed happier in his work. There was also a new contemplative mood about him. I would catch him gazing at Grís' *El Guitarrista,* which hung above his bed, or looking up out of one of the large windows in his workroom, almost as if he was searching for something in the cobalt-blue sky. There were times I saw him talk to himself, laugh, and move about the room, acting out a scene much like the way actors rehearse their lines.

"Don't think I'm crazy if you hear me laughing or talking to myself," he told me one day after I returned with the morning's mail and caught him standing by the window laughing heartily and talking to himself. "I'm just remembering, reliving events related to what I'm writing." He was working on the African safari book at the time, and I suppose certain passages made him remember humorous moments.

On another morning I went to his workroom to retrieve the breakfast tray. He met me by the door, pencil in hand.

"Did you hear that? What was it?" he asked with a smirk.

"Quails. A couple just flew by."

Papa then went into great detail about the quails' early-morning ritual of passing by his window on their way down to the pool to drink.

The following morning I woke earlier than usual and headed to the quails' watering place. At the terrace steps, I heard a quail call followed by the quick flight of the covey. The birds flew to a safe distance and disappeared in the vegetation. I walked over to where they had been drinking. It was then that I noticed small pebbles bouncing off my feet. I looked up and saw Papa Hemingway, in long khaki pants and shirt, hiding behind the bamboo.

"Not like that. You'll never be able to get close to them," Hemingway said, laughing and shaking his head. "Even though you tried not to make any noise, you came in from the front. If you're going to be a good hunter, you have to surprise your prey, not have the prey surprise you." He told me that I should have been there at least thirty minutes earlier and then taken cover. He went into great detail of how four quails arrived first, two old couples. They were always the first. One of the old males let the rest know it was safe. After drinking water, one couple left and headed toward the tower to post guard. The other couple posted guard on the opposite direction. Then a larger and younger group came to drink.

"I knew you were approaching without even seeing you," he said.

"I wanted to confirm what you told me yesterday," I said.

"I knew you would get up and look for the quails this morning. I saw the look of curiosity you had when you left my room."

Early one morning, not long after the lesson with the quails, Hemingway was waiting for me on the terrace when I returned from the pueblo with the morning's mail.

"Nothing wrong, muchacho," he reassured me. "I was just anxious for you to return from the pueblo. I'm sure a circus came to town last night." He saw my surprise. "You forget I'm a hunter. I caught the scent of the gaticos last night, and this morning I heard them roar. I bet you were not aware a circus had come to town last night?"

I told him that the postmaster had told me this morning. I knew Papa would ask me about the circus, so I had gone to investigate before heading back with the mail. I told him that the circus tent was full of patches from different materials and colors. There were two lions, one with a great black mane, and a younger one, a lioness. All three looked skinny. There were also two Chinese crested dogs, a pinto pony, and far too many employees for such a small circus.

"I'm working well this morning. When I finish around noon, we'll go take a look at those 'kitties,'" Papa said on his way back into the house.

A little after noon, he finished working and told Mary we were going to check out the circus. The two of us walked down the pine path to the entrance of the Finca. We didn't have to walk far. The circus was close to the gate. The first person we met when we got there was Moralito, the owner, who immediately realized whom he was speaking to and gave us a tour.

Papa and I observed the three lions, each in separate cages. "You were right," he whispered to me. "They look hungry."

Moralito, overhearing Papa's comment explained his situation. He knew that he had too many employees for a small circus. He'd hired employees from another circus that went bankrupt a couple of months earlier. Moralito said that they were good people and didn't want to see them out of work. He also said that his biggest attraction was the lions, and he had to pay the tamer after every performance—and pay him well.

"Don't worry. If you ever need a tamer, I can come and tame the lions for you. I hope next time we see each other the gaticos are better fed," Hemingway said jokingly.

Later that afternoon, I went for the mail. Mancebo, the postmaster, was happy to see me and said that he didn't know el señor Hemingway was also a lion tamer. He said that Moralito had been announcing all over the pueblo that Ernest Hemingway would tame the lions in tonight's performance. "See it with your own eyes," the postmaster said. "Moralito is still out there."

I left the post office and followed the sound of the drums. I ran until I met up with the noisy procession.

"Attention pueblo of San Francisco de Paula! One night only for an exclusive performance. Mr. Ernest Hemingway, the famous American writer, will perform in a special spectacular performance, as the lion tamer, risking his life in front of fierce man-eating beasts!" Moralito, dressed with top hat and coattails, announced this through a megaphone. He was followed by a small parade of circus performers.

A couple of people stopped me and asked if it was true. I said it was a mistake. I didn't know whether to stop Moralito from announcing this or hurry back to the house and tell Papa what was happening. The damage had been done already. The entire town had heard the announcement. And soon it would reach Hemingway. I decided to head back to the house.

I ran all the way up to the Finca. I looked for Hemingway in his room, the living room, Mary's room. Mary told me Papa had gone down for a swim. I hurried to the pool.

"What's wrong, muchacho?" Papa asked, noticing how nervous I was. He got out of the pool and wrapped a towel around his waist. I explained what had happened. "Of course! He wants to fill the circus using my name. We all took it as a joke. I was never serious about entering the cage with the gaticos."

"I'll make him take it back," I said.

"No, then people will say I backed out. For now, let's not do anything. I'm going up to speak to Miss Mary. I will explain what has happened." He went to Mary's room.

I went to the pantry to prepare the food for the cats and dogs. A couple of minutes later I heard Hemingway and Mary arguing. I stopped to listen, to try to catch any English word I could. Papa wouldn't seriously consider entering the lion's cage, would he? The arguing continued. I went to the living room and arranged the magazines and newspapers. Mary came out of her room, tears in her eyes. She signaled for me to follow her to the pantry.

"At all costs we cannot allow Papa to go to the circus and get inside the lion's cage," she said, a desperate tone in her voice and tears spilling from her eyes.

I found Papa in his bathroom holding the whiskey bottle full of lion lard. He asked me to help him get the lion lard out of the bottle. I went to the closet and got a wire hanger. Hemingway took it and scraped out some lard into an empty cup. He said that we should rub the lion lard on our bodies in order to smell like a lion when we went inside the cage. At this point I realized that he was dead serious and that he was relishing this challenge. And not only was he serious about going into the lion's cage, but he expected me to go in as well! The blood left my face, and I was numb for a few seconds.

"Isn't that more dangerous, smelling like lions?" I asked nervously.

"No. Why? I don't think so," he said.

"Miss Mary is very concerned. She asked me to talk you out of it."

"You're telling me you won't accompany me either!"

"No, Papa," I hesitated. "I'll go with you." Somehow I had agreed to step into the lion's cage with him. Was he testing me? I didn't want him to think I wouldn't back him up. I didn't want him to think I was a coward. If he was going to step into the lion's cage, so would I.

He must have seen the look on my face. "You will not enter the cage," he said, changing his mind. But you'll be close, and it will be better if you smelled like a lion." I was very relieved.

He said that he wouldn't take a gun with him into the cage because he didn't shoot caged animals. That was not honorable. In Africa he hunted lions in the wild, and in this situation he would have all the advantage. "There is a vast difference between a lion tamer with a whip and a man entering the cage with a firearm," he told me. I wanted to take a firearm with me to back him up, but he insisted against it. "You realize it's up to you and me. We have to show our faces tonight." He paused and thought for a while. "Relax muchacho and tell Miss Mary not to worry. I'll show up and play along with this sick joke, and tomorrow we'll be the ones laughing about the whole thing."

Hemingway dressed in a pair of khaki pants and shirt. He also wore his favorite old leather boots, the same boots he'd worn on the last safari. Mary, who came along to support and witness the spectacle, also wore her safari outfit. I stuck with my white guayabera, black pants, and black moccasins.

Together, we left the house and walked down the pine tree–lined path. Mary held onto Hemingway's arm, and he laughed and joked about the whole thing. We exited the Finca and followed the noise and the people. As we approached the circus, we could hear people murmuring, "It's true, it's true! El americano came down. He is going to enter the lions' cage. The lions are going to eat him alive." Someone rushed up to me and asked if Hemingway was a lion tamer. I didn't respond. We kept on walking.

We entered the circus through the main entrance and saw that the performance had already begun. There was a clown holding hoops and a pinto pony trotting inside a small ring, on its back was a small Chinese crested dog jumping through the hoops each time the pony passed the clown. We saw a man dressed in a lion tamer's suit and walked over to him.

"Gonzalo. You are the famous lion tamer of this circus!" Hemingway shook hands with the man. The man greeted Papa with great enthusiasm and told us that he'd been working with Moralito ever since the Montarvo circus went under.

Papa explained what Moralito had done. Concerned, Gonzalo urged Hemingway not to go into the cage with the lions. He'd come in from Havana by coincidence, and when he heard about tonight's performance he decided to get dressed and wait. Papa asked Gonzalo to help him get even with Moralito for playing this sick joke and for using his name to sell tickets. "This afternoon, we all had a bad time at the

Finca, but tomorrow it will be Moralito who will have a bad time," Hemingway said to Gonzalo and looked at us. Mary and I smiled back at him.

The clown finished his performance with the pony and dogs and walked over to us laughing, wildly waving his arms, and jumping around. Not until then did we realize that the clown was Moralito.

"I'm here for tonight's performance as the lion tamer," Hemingway said dead seriously, looking straight into Moralito's eyes. The clown stopped jumping and became motionless in horror. Papa told him that, since Moralito had advertised it all over town, he had to go into the cage. These people were his friends and neighbors, and he didn't want them to think that he was a liar and a coward. "The pueblo came to see how the lions maul Hemingway, not to see Hemingway tame the lions!" Papa said raising his voice.

Desperate, Moralito pleaded several times for Hemingway to reconsider and that he knew it had been a sick joke. He didn't want an awful tragedy to happen. Papa ordered Moralito to schedule the lion's act immediately, because he was a very busy man and would like to go home and have dinner—"Unless of course, the lions have me for dinner," Hemingway said with a smirk. Mary and I looked at each other with eyes wide open. How far was Papa going to take the charade?

"Tomorrow my driver will stop for you and this gentleman at 12:00 P.M. sharp," Papa said to Moralito and pointing to Gonzalo, as if he didn't know the man. "And don't forget to bring all the money you make from tonight's performance. We'll divide the profits into four equal parts: one part for you, one for me, and the other two parts for my assistants, my wife, Miss Mary, and René Villarreal, mi hombre de confianza." It was a sad thing to see a clown almost in tears.

Gonzalo advised Papa to stay outside close to the door of the cage and to open it in case things got difficult for him.

"I'm going in with you. I'll stay close," Papa said in a calm voice. Mary and I looked at each other. There was no point in arguing at that moment. Hemingway was determined to go into the cage, and arguing with him would make matters worse.

Gonzalo then gave Papa careful instructions on what to do once they got inside the cage. "I have complete faith in you," Hemingway said to Gonzalo.

Mary stayed close to the cage, looking out for any sign of trouble. I walked around the cage and found another angle to watch from.

Gonzalo picked up a chair and a whip. Hemingway picked up another chair, and together they entered the cage. Gonzalo immediately cracked the whip in front of the larger, more aggressive beast. Hemingway stood very close to Gonzalo's left and kept his eye on the smaller lion. The crowd was dead quiet in disbelief. Ernest Hemingway had actually gone into the lions' cage. The large lion furiously clawed, knocking the chair from Gonzalo's hand. The crowd jumped. Gonzalo cracked the whip in the lion's face several times, making him retreat. Hemingway gave his chair to Gonzalo, who told him to walk to the door and leave the cage. Hemingway slowly made his way to the entrance of the cage without turning his back to the lions. He closed the door behind him. Gonzalo quickly finished his performance and left the cage. The crowd went wild. Gonzalo took a couple of bows while Hemingway waved to the cheering crowd.

The following day, around noon, Juan picked up Moralito and Gonzalo and drove them to the Finca. Hemingway greeted them in the living room with a martini in hand.

"Buenos días amigos," he said smiling and shaking hands with the two men. "Would you like a beer, rum, a shot of whiskey. A martini perhaps?"

Moralito declined and remained tense. Gonzalo accepted a Cuba libre. "Have a drink hombre," Hemingway said. Moralito confessed that he'd not been able to sleep all night long. "More reason to have a drink. Venga hombre!" Hemingway insisted.

Moralito decided on a martini. I finished mixing the Cuba libre for Gonzalo and then made the martini. I gave the drink to Moralito, who drank it down in one gulp.

"Hombre! You have to slow down with those. If you drink like that you won't be able to hold another. Pace yourself and enjoy it," Hemingway said, relishing the moment. "Well, let's get down to business. How much did you make last night?" Hemingway asked very seriously.

Moralito was as pale as a bedsheet. He said that if his financial situation wasn't so bad, he'd pick up shop and leave immediately. "I made more money last night than I've seen in a long time, and I have to share it with you," Moralito said, visibly shaken. "I didn't even count the money, Don Ernesto. All of it is inside the bag just as the ticketmaster gave it to me. My last hope to better the situation of my circus is in that bag, and now the money is not even mine. I wanted to buy a new top, a couple of more animals, pay my employees," he said in despair.

"Write down what you think all of that would cost and print your name clearly on the bottom of the sum. Also have Gonzalo print his full name," Hemingway said, handing Moralito a piece of paper and a pencil.

Papa then took the paper into the library and came out a few minutes later with two envelopes. "This check is a gift so you can improve your circus. You can keep all the proceeds from last night's performance." Hemingway handed Moralito one envelope. "Gonzalo, this check is for your help."

Moralito's face completely changed. He thanked Hemingway several times, vigorously shaking his hand. Gonzalo also thanked Hemingway.

"Never use my name again for promotion or you will have to deal with my attorneys. I command $10,000 for public appearances," Papa said smiling. "Relax hombre! Let's toast together."

I prepared four shot glasses with rum, and we all toasted the lion tamer.

BOXING HEMINGWAY

Hemingway was trying very hard to maintain the strict diet prescribed by his Spanish doctor. But it was hard for a man who was used to drinking and living the way he did to settle for just one glass of wine with lunch and dinner. I remember the days when he and Mary finished two bottles of wine at lunch and two more at dinner. And while he followed his diet, he also stopped having his Tom Collins or martinis after lunch and only on occasion had a glass of wine.

During September of 1955, Hemingway told me that his friend and lawyer Alfred Rice was coming to stay for a short time. He would stay in the Venetian Room. The bungalow was reserved for George Brown, who was also coming and would be a witness to Papa's new will.

"I hope George Brown has a good time here," he said. "You'll like him. He's a real gentleman. Very knowledgeable of boxing. He has a gymnasium in New York City and has trained some great champions. He hits hard, and even though he's an old man, he's still dangerous in the ring."

On September 17, 1955, Lola Richards, Mary's maid, and George Brown and I served as witnesses for Hemingway's new will and testament. After taking care of some other legal matters, Mr. Rice headed back to the States. George Brown stayed behind to enjoy life at the Finca.

Early one morning Hemingway asked me to tell Mr. Brown to join a group of us by the pool and then pick up the boxing gloves and head gear. On the way to the bungalow, I passed Mario Sánchez, who was carrying the heavy medicine ball Kid Tunero had given me as a gift.

Hemingway and I often worked out with the medicine ball. It seemed to alleviate his back pains. As I walked back down to the pool with the gear, I met up with Juan.

"Qué pasa, Kid Vigía? Is there boxing again at the Finca?" he joked. I told him that Papa wanted the gloves and gear by the pool and had asked me to tell George Brown to meet us there and that Mario was also waiting. "Mario was good in his youth, but you know he's punch-drunk," Juan said laughing.

I told him that I was thinking of sparring with George Brown. "The old man is in top form. I see him exercise every morning. He may give me a good spar," I said with a cocky attitude.

Juan and I walked to the pool and met up with Papa and Mario. Once Mr. Brown appeared, we all walked over to the tennis court. It had been a long time since Hemingway and I had sparred. Mario was ready to spar. He put on a pair of gloves and immediately started to shadow-box. Papa told Mario that I was to spar only with him. Papa knew that Mario would try to fight hard, and he didn't want anyone to get hurt during the sparring session.

"We'll do three rounds," Hemingway said, putting on a pair of gloves. "Then, I will finish the session with Mr. Brown—if he wishes to fight me," Hemingway said looking at George Brown and smiling out the corner of his mouth. Mr. Brown smiled back.

Papa and I touched our left gloves and started circling each other. We knew each other's moves from all the years we had lightly sparred. Hemingway jabbed, trying to corner me to his right. I moved to avoid the trap and stayed away from his left jab. When I was a child he took it easier on me and taught me how to throw punches and weave in and out. Once I got older, he increased the pressure. But we never really broke to a full boxing match. We respected each other.

We continued circling each other now. He moved well, avoiding my punches, and signaled me to throw more. We finished the three rounds and touched gloves. I felt great. Papa was sweating and somewhat out of breath.

Papa and George Brown then sparred a couple of rounds. They hit each other a lot harder than he and I did. I guess they had things to prove to each other. We agreed that the following morning I would spar with George Brown. "No lastimes al muchacho (don't hurt the boy)," Papa said to Mr. Brown.

"Just a couple of rounds," George Brown said.

As we walked back to the house, Papa whispered to me, "He's an old devil and knows a lot of tricks. Be careful with him."

The next morning, George Brown and I met by ourselves on the tennis court. We touched gloves and started measuring each other up.

"Don't hold back," he said as he circled me. "I won't hurt you only because Papa asked me not to."

At that point my ego had been challenged, and I was determined to show the old man what I was capable of. I launched three fast jabs at his forehead. He avoided them by simply moving his head to one side. I crossed with a strong hard right and again missed my target. For three rounds I threw my best punches and as many as I could. Some of the punches landed, but none were good enough to hurt him. With great skill, George Brown avoided every single combination I threw. In the last seconds of the rounds, he'd clinch and lean his weight on me. I was younger and faster, yet I wasn't able to land a single good solid punch on the man. The only punches he threw were to my shoulders and biceps. They were fast and hard punches. In the fourth and last round my arms were so tired that I couldn't keep my hands up. George Brown danced in front of me, faked with his left, and then threw a hard right. The punch stopped inches from my face. He then threw a couple of jabs opening my now-weak guard and another hard right to my face again stopping only inches away, followed by a couple of fast jabs to my jaw.

"I can knock you out right now," he said, dancing around me with vigor.

I took a deep breath and threw a hard right. He avoided it with ease. It had been my last desperate attempt to reach him. I wasn't hurt—except for my bruised ego—just utterly exhausted. I had no doubt in my mind that Brown could have easily knocked me out. He had proven it. But he had been a gentleman and stopped the punches short.

That morning Mr. George Brown gave me a boxing lesson I would never forget. He was a master in the ring and a true gentleman as well. "You're strong and fast, but you've a lot to learn," he said trying to make me feel better. I nodded and didn't say a word. I picked up the boxing gear and walked back to the bungalow with him. He said he was going for a swim.

Later that afternoon I told Papa of my encounter with Mr. George Brown. He understood that my pride had been hurt. "I told you Mr. Brown was good. He's good enough to give any decent heavyweight a run for his money." He smiled and patted my back. I tried to smile, but I couldn't. "Tomorrow, Mario can massage your shoulders and arms. You'll be fine in a couple of days," he said. I didn't know whether he meant my shoulders or my pride. George Brown became one of the best friends I made in the years I worked at the Finca Vigía.

I got to meet a few boxing legends during my time at the Finca. Rocky Marciano made a brief visit. He was not very tall, but I could see the power in his stocky frame and was mesmerized by his thick, muscular neck that could certainly take anyone's punch. Gene Tunney, the former heavyweight champion who won the title from Jack Dempsey, came for lunch with his wife one day. Papa and Tunney drank heavily that afternoon, and it wasn't long before they were exchanging light punches in the dining room. It all seemed harmless enough until one of them let go and punched a bit too hard. Then it quickly escalated into a grudge match. Mary ran to me and asked me to break up the fight. I took a step toward them and for a moment wondered how a 147-pound man could stop two 200-plus-pound men—never mind that one of them was a former heavyweight champion of the world. And never mind that they were both drunk. Somehow, Mary, Tunney's wife, and I were able to stop the fight. A few seconds later they shook hands and resumed their drinking and amicable conversation.

In early 1956, production of the film version of *The Old Man and the Sea* was under way. Leland Hayward and his lovely wife, Slim Hawks, came to stay at the Finca. They were followed by the star of the movie, Spencer Tracy, who was followed by Katherine Hepburn. The two actors dined and drank up a storm at the Finca.

Hemingway was not too pleased with Mr. Tracy's appearance. The actor refused to exercise and presented himself for the role out of shape. It took only a little time for friction to develop between Hemingway and Tracy. Hemingway often commented on Mr. Tracy's appearance, saying he looked more like an old, rich, overweight actor than an old starving fisherman.

The Warner Brothers film crew scouted the neighboring shores and villages to film the scenes of the old fisherman's village described in the book. The small village of Boca de Jaruco was the location that came the closest to resembling the site in the novella. The crew built shacks and planted more palm trees to obtain the "authentic" setting.

But Hemingway, along with several friends, as well as the film crew, was not having any luck catching a good-sized marlin off Cuban waters, and they decided to try their luck in Cayo Blanco, Peru. There, Hemingway finally caught the great fish they had been after for the footage of the film. He sent me a photograph of him standing next to the great 1,554-pound fish. On the photo he wrote, "Finally got my prized marlin, Papa." He looked very happy in the photo. The postmaster told me the picture was definitely a collector's item. I thought so as well. I'm so sorry to have lost it.

TURBULENT TIMES

Fidel Alejandro Castro Ruz was born on a sugar plantation in what is today the province of Holguín. This illegitimate son of a prosperous Galician immigrant attended a Jesuit boarding school during his early years and eventually graduated with a law degree from the University of Havana. His strong criticism of and opposition to dictator Fulgencio Batista's economic, social, and political policies led him on a rebellious attack on the Moncada army barracks in Santiago on July 26, 1953. The attack failed, and most of the rebels involved were killed or captured. Castro was captured and given a trial and sentenced to 15 years in prison. However, after serving only two years, he was given amnesty by Batista and went into exile in Mexico, where he met Che Guevara. Returning to Cuba in 1956, the revolutionaries hid in the Sierra Maestra mountains, and from there they gained support among the youth, the farmers, and the working poor.

By 1957, the political situation in Cuba had become unbearable. University students and much of the young population were unhappy with the corrupt Batista government. The huge division between the rich and poor and American special interests in Cuba were causes the revolutionaries took on. All over the island, there were demonstrations and small revolts. Eventually the crisis escalated and became more violent.

Even in the small pueblo of San Francisco de Paula we felt the violent waves of the changing times. Almost every week we heard rumors of a young man found badly beaten, or dead. These badly mutilated bodies usually surfaced a couple of days after an unexplained disappearance, found in ditches or on the side of some secluded road.

Others were found with a shot in the back of the head, execution style. Anti-Batista sentiment grew by the day, and the young men who were known to be active against the government fled to Sierra Maestra to join Fidel Castro. The ones who stayed in their hometowns ran the risk of becoming casualties. The reality of the situation reached San Francisco de Paula and me when the bodies of friends I had known since childhood and who worked in La Cerveceria Hatuey were found tortured and mutilated.

Early one day I was in the living room when I saw my brother Luis walking up the steps of the house. He wore his uniform from the mineral water company and carried his cap in his hand. I met him outside. "What's wrong?!" I asked, alarmed. He said that our brother didn't come home last night. I knew it was Helio. According to Luis, Chela, Helio's wife, had come this morning and told the family that he had not returned from work the night before. At first she thought he was working extra hours, but she became concerned as she thought of what happened to Guido Pérez, one of the young men found dead after an unexplained disappearance.

We knew my oldest brother was a womanizer, an adventurer, and he liked to pick fights in bars. But he had never been political. None of us had ever been political. But who knew what kind of a situation he might have gotten himself in? Luis said that our mother was very nervous because this morning she heard on the radio about a body that was found in an abandoned lot in Havana, and the description of the body matched Helio's.

The front door of the house opened and Hemingway walked out to meet us. "Something wrong Luis? Are you in trouble?" Papa was concerned. We explained the situation and our fears. At that moment Juan walked up from the garage and greeted us. "Juan, take them to a morgue in Havana to identify a body," Papa instructed.

We arrived at the morgue and went to view the corpse. The body was badly beaten and nearly unrecognizable. But we knew it wasn't Helio. The fingers and hands were broken, and the chest showed numerous stab wounds. There was a single bullet wound to the chest. It looked like a .22 caliber wound probably shot at point-blank range, or quema ropa, as people called it. The man's testicles and penis had been burned. I had heard rumors that torturers would tie the naked victim to a chair that had no bottom, place a burner under the chair, and slowly increase the fire until the genitals burned.

We looked at the body for what seem an eternity. We didn't speak to each other. I felt so sorry for the family of the tortured man. It wasn't enough he was killed, but they had to destroy him. I am sure many people who had been tortured and killed had nothing to do with the revolution. Their innocence had cost them their lives.

Juan waited for us by the car. He looked at us when we came out, and I shook my head to let him know it was not our brother. We got in the car and drove back to the Finca in silence. We stopped by our mother's house to let her know it was not her son, our brother, in the Havana morgue. Later, we found out that Helio had stayed out drinking. He got a good scolding from his wife and the rest of the family.

A couple of weeks after this scare, in the middle of the night we were awakened by the frantic barking of the dogs. I knew from their bark that whoever had approached the Finca was not a friend. As I got out of bed, I heard Hemingway get up. He knew I was awake as well. He stamped his feet a couple of times, alerting me to go upstairs.

"René, are you awake!?" Mary called out from her window. "Come up, quick!" About nine armed soldiers were coming up the steps to the house. By the time she and I reached the living room, Hemingway had the door open halfway and was talking to them.

"What are you looking for?! What do you want on my property?!" He was loud and upset.

"We're looking for jovenes revolucionarios. We have information that they're hiding in the vicinity," said the lieutenant. The soldiers had come in two jeeps; one vehicle was left parked by the gate of the Finca and the other was in front of Steinhart's house. The men carried rifles and wore the khaki uniform of the Cuban army. They looked tired and reeked of booze.

Papa ordered, "There are no revolucionarios here. Leave my property immediately." The soldiers hesitated for a moment then turned around and left. The dogs followed the men. We heard their barks grow fainter as the soldiers walked away from the house.

"Let me make sure they leave the Finca," I said opening the door, ready to follow.

"Don't. They might shoot." Papa grabbed my arm. The dogs stopped barking all of a sudden.

"Something is wrong," I said.

"Esos hijos de putas probably wanted money to get more drunk!" Hemingway said, still visibly upset.

We stayed up for an hour and then went back to bed. As I lay on my bed, I knew something bad had happened that night, something awful.

The following morning, on my way to serve Hemingway his breakfast, I saw all the dogs by the kitchen stairs except for Machakos. I told Papa that one of our dogs was missing. He said, "Before you get the mail, search around where esos hijos de putas walked down to the entrance."

I followed the same path the soldiers had taken the night before and found the body of Machakos hidden behind the trees. His head had been smashed in. One of the soldiers must have hit him with the butt of a rifle. That's why the other dogs stopped barking. Filled with rage, I walked up to the house. Hemingway saw me coming up and met me outside. From the look on my face, he knew it was bad news. "They killed him," I said. "They smashed his head."

"Those animals!" Papa was infuriated. "When they walked up to the house last night, I felt like shooting at them!"

Machakos had been a pup when Papa and Mary had returned from the safari in 1954. Mary named him and his brother Tatos. She said they were names of places they had stayed in Africa. We buried Machakos where we found his body. Hemingway thought it would be appropriate to bury him where the dog died defending his home. Papa and Mary tried to get the culprits punished. They even asked for assistance from the American embassy, but the soldiers went unpunished.

New York Times reporter Herbert Matthews visited the Finca Vigía that year. He was an old friend of Hemingway's who had also covered the Spanish Civil War. Mr. Matthews was in Cuba to interview Fidel Castro in La Sierra Maestra. He told Hemingway more about the political and military unrest. He said that Castro and his men had a strong following and were well armed and that Batista should be concerned.

As it became clear a revolution was ahead, Hemingway set out in the *Pilar* with Gregorio and tossed overboard a few firearms he stored in the boat. The night he came back, he seemed relieved to have gotten rid of the weapons. He didn't want either side getting ahold of them. The guns were better off in the bottom of the ocean. Papa said that he was too old and too tired to be a part of any of it.

THE FAMILY MAN

It wasn't until early March of 1957 that Papa and Mary finally met Fanny. We had been dating for three years and been engaged for about a year. Papa was delighted with my fiancée. He liked her long black hair and beautiful smile. On meeting her, he smiled and silently gave me his approval. "Cuida bien a mi hijo cubano," he said to her as the three of us posed for a photograph.

The following morning when I took the mail to his room, he said, "Your fiancée seems like a wonderful girl. You know you can move to the bungalow if you want. That way you'll always be close to her."

"Thank you Papa, but we already rented an apartment very close. It's just outside the Finca. I can see the pine tree path from our window."

"You should take the bungalow and save on the rent. Miss Mary and I always want you to be close. You can always move into the house when we're away." I knew that he meant it.

A couple of days later, on March 10, Fanny and I traveled to Santa Clara, her hometown, and were married. After many failed relationships, I had finally met the honest and hardworking woman my father had advised me to find.

The first time I saw Fanny was on a Sunday afternoon back in 1953 when she walked past my house. Papa and Mary had recently left for Africa, and I had begun my boxing career. I was playing with my dog in front of my family's home. He was a large German shepherd named Diablo (after the sidekick of one of my favorite childhood characters, El Fantasma, whose comic books I read as a young boy and movie serials I watched on the weekends). She asked me to hold the dog until she passed. It was obvious she was afraid of him. As she walked by, I contemplated her long black, wavy hair, her dark eyes, and her shapely figure. She ignored me completely and continued on her way. I had not seen her before around the pueblo and thought that she was either visiting or had recently moved here.

From time to time I saw her around the pueblo, but I didn't have the opportunity to speak to her until one late afternoon when I went to Bebo and Nino's bar for a beer and saw her waiting for the bus in La Carretera Central. She was with two other young ladies, who turned out to be her sisters, and they had luggage with them. I gathered some courage to approach them and introduced myself. I then asked if they needed any help. Fanny quickly and firmly declined. I asked what bus they were waiting for, and she told me "the Santiago-Havana." I told her that that was not the correct route, that she must be waiting for Havana-Santiago, since she was in the province of Havana heading to Santiago de Cuba. After adamantly correcting me several times and not giving in, she was elbowed by one of her sisters, a signal to stop arguing with me. I waited until the bus arrived and helped the three of them load their luggage in the side cabin of the bus. As the bus departed, I was intrigued and amused at the stubbornness and feisty personality of the beautiful young señorita.

On April 2, 1954, the Day of San Francisco de Paula, the pueblo hosted the annual saint fair and procession. My brothers and I participated in the horse-riding competition, where a rider had to gallop at full speed in a straight run and hook a ring with a stick. I later learned that Fanny and her sisters watched the competition and were amazed by the speed with which I switched horses to ride on both the red *and* blue teams. That was the topic of conversation the next time I saw her. I explained that it was my twin brother riding his horse for the red team and that we were dressed alike. She didn't believe me at all, and it wasn't until I introduced him to her one day that she did not think of me as a liar.

After I started dating Fanny, I found out that the family had moved to the pueblo after the oldest daughter, Zoila, married and moved to the city of Havana. Their mother, Zoila Rosa Rodríguez Vizcaino, came with the other four girls and two younger boys. The father stayed in Santa Clara to work at his barbershop, visiting whenever he could. They were a large family of humble means. Zoila was the oldest of the daughters, followed by Marta, Silvia, Fanny, Cristina, and the two much younger sons, Rafael and Miguel. The daughters lived at home and worked in different jobs to contribute to the household. Fanny worked at Los Panesitos, a small sandwich shop about a mile west of where we lived on La Carretera Central.

A good friend of mine, Lazaro Carballo, began dating Marta. The four of us went out dancing at clubs in Havana, and at times we gathered at the Finca when Papa and Mary were away. We spent some great times by the pool sampling some of the Finca's champagne and wines. But mostly we spent a lot of time at the girls' house, which was about four blocks from mine. Lazaro and I visited with the family and enjoyed terrific comida criolla prepared by her mother and the girls. It wasn't long before I fell in love with Fanny and knew that she was the woman I was going to marry.

Late in 1957, we had our firstborn, a beautiful boy we named Eduardo, after her father. He was born ill and died a couple of days later. Fanny and I were devastated. We had waited eagerly for the birth of the child. We loved children and wanted a large family.

The day of my son's burial, I carried the small white coffin on my shoulder. Family members followed. I heard Fanny weep behind me, my sister, the other aunts and uncles, and the baby's grandmothers. I walked slowly, my eyes welling with tears. Luis told me sometime later that Juan had parked the stationwagon by the gate of the Finca and Hemingway had gotten out of the car and walked behind us. Papa walked all the way up to the little church on the hill but didn't go to the cemetery. Papa never approached me. He didn't want to face me. I understood why

Confused and still grieving, I went back to work two days after we buried Eduardito. That first morning when I took Hemingway his breakfast, he asked sternly, "What are you doing? Shouldn't you be home with your wife?"

"But I have responsibilities."

"Yes, to your wife and to yourself."

"I can't stand being home," I said tearfully.

"You have to be with her. Go home!" He was adamant. "Don't let this come between you. Time will heal the pain." So I went home and consoled Fanny, and she consoled me.

A few months later, Fanny and I moved to another house off the Carretera Central. We couldn't bear to live in the apartment with the memories of the baby. Soon Fanny became pregnant, and nine months later, on September 10, 1958, René Jr. was born. My son looked just like me. Hemingway and Mary carried and played with René Jr. Papa took him in his arms and showed him the safari trophies on the walls. I was a proud father. He was a strong, healthy, beautiful boy. But even knowing this, for a year I lived with the fear that he would be taken from me.

A little more than a year after René Jr. arrived, we were blessed with Rodolfo, another strong and healthy boy. He was born on October 6, 1959. A couple years later came Fanny, our first daughter, on April 29, 1963, and Raúl followed on July 16, 1964. Then we had the baby of the family almost as a Christmas present. Martha was born on December 18, 1965.

It was difficult managing fatherhood and dealing with my responsibilities at the Finca, but every opportunity I had to stop by the house during the day I took it. After serving lunch at the Finca, during siesta time, I walked home to be with my family.

LA REVOLUCIÓN

On New Year's Eve 1958, Batista fled Cuba and Fidel Castro and his revolucionarios took over the capital. The news of the triumph of the revolution had people dancing and parading in the streets through the night and well into the next morning. Those who had been neutral all of a sudden became the most avid supporters of Fidel Castro. My family had been apolitical, and we remained neutral. We had seen dictators come and go, and there was nothing different about this one, or so we thought.

Papa Hemingway and Mary were in Idaho at the time, where they had purchased their Sun Valley ranch. From Ketchum, Hemingway spoke to newspaper reporters favorably of the young revolution. He was quoted as saying, "I believe in the historical necessity for the Cuban revolution, and I believe in its long-range aims. I do not wish to discuss personalities or day to day problems." During his life in Cuba, Hemingway had lived under one dictator and another. He knew how the abusive, criminal, and corrupt Batista government had strained the pueblo's tolerance and patience. Hemingway himself had experienced it that night when the soldiers entered his property and killed one of his dogs. I believe that Papa hoped that he and Mary would still be able to live in his beloved Cuba under the new government.

That year was filled with many unknowns for Cuba. While Castro was very popular with the masses, already there were those displeased with the direction the country was heading.

A few weeks into the new year, a large group from the pueblo who had become avid suporters of la revolución and had established a local assembly came up to the Finca. They wanted me to give them all of Hemingway's firearms to protect and maintain la revolución fuerte, a strong revolution. I told them that the revolution had triumphed already and that there was no need for such action. The weapons in the house were for hunting and not warfare and that they would only take the arms over my dead body. I knew most of the dozen or so men in the group. I knew their families, and their families knew mine. The mob left without any trouble. Afterward I spoke to Papa on the telephone. He told me that if they came back I was to give them the arms without a fight and that Juan should provide them the stationwagon if need be. "If something happens, hold on there as long as you can. I'll get you out." His voice revealed concern. The next morning, I summoned the men to the Finca and handed over the weapons, which were returned a couple of days later without a single one of them being fired. The stationwagon was never used.

When Papa and Mary returned to Cuba on March 29, 1959, a busload of people from San Francisco de Paula went to greet them at the Havana airport. The man who had won the Nobel Prize in literature was returning to his home in Cuba after having praised the young revolution. Now Hemingway was an even bigger hero to the Cuban people. The crowd presented Hemingway with a Cuban flag. When he was handed the flag, Papa hugged and kissed it. The photographers were distracted and didn't capture the gesture. The people of San Francisco de Paula applauded their friend. The photographers asked Hemingway to repeat the gesture. He said with annoyance, "Soy escritor no actor. Señores he besado esta bandera con sinceridad (I'm a writer not an actor. Gentlemen, I've kissed this flag with sincerity)." The people of San Francisco de Paula applauded once more with greater enthusiasm.

Hemingway and Mary settled back into life at the Finca Vigía. They had seen hints of anti-Americanism surfacing before the triumph of the revolution, so they made their life as low-key as possible. Although Fidel Castro had promised that any American who had been a friend and not an exploiter of the Cuban people had nothing to fear, still there was an uneasiness in the air, and Hemingway sensed it. Papa was loved by the Cuban people, but in countries where governmental coups come and go, there is always a chance of the tides turning from sunrise to sunset. Papa knew about the aftermath of revolution and that there would be much blood spilled even yet. There was a lot of resentment and vengeful sentiments toward Batista's officials, soldiers, and secret police. Those who were known to have tortured and abused their power were tried and executed in public. Other trials and swift executions followed—and not only for Batista's men but for people who were, or could eventually become, threats to the revolution.

In April Hemingway and Mary traveled to Spain for the summer. Hemingway wanted to relive his early days there and work in a different setting. For some time he had been contemplating revising his book *Death in the Afternoon*. Papa and Mary stayed at the Consula in Málaga, at the home of his friend John Davis. I was instructed to send all the correspondence there. At the Consula, they were joined by A. E. Hotchner and others for the corridas, which promised to be interesting with Luis Miguel Dominguín returning from early retirement and competing against his brother-in-law, the younger and highly regarded Antonio Ordóñez. Hemingway eagerly followed the matadors, but he preferred the younger and more endearing man. Throughout the summer I received letters from Papa telling me of the bullfights and his praises for Antonio Ordóñez. At some point during the mano-a-mano, news of the corridas captured the interest of American magazines.

Mary returned alone to Cuba in September of 1959. She said that Papa would soon arrive and that the Finca needed to be prepared for the guests. I sensed there was something wrong, but she would not speak to me about it. Hemingway arrived in Cuba that November with the Ordóñezes.

"We had an unforgettable time," Papa told me, smiling. "We visited many ferias following Antonio Ordóñez, Luis Miguel Dominguín, and other great matadors. It made me think of the times when I wrote *The Sun Also Rises* and *Death in the Afternoon*." In his eyes I could see that he had succeded in recapturing some of the great times.

Antonio Ordóñez and his beautiful wife, Carmen, stayed in the bungalow for less than two weeks. They sunbathed and enjoyed the tranquility and quiet of the Finca Vigía and were unbothered by the aftermath of a revolution. Then they were off to the States with Hemingway to meet with Mary in the new house in Ketchum.

Upon Papa and Mary's return to the Finca from Ketchum in January of 1960, Mary told me that we had to do our best to get him back on the strict diet. While he was in Spain, Papa had abandoned his diet and forgotten about his high blood pressure. Sixty was not an advanced age by any means, but Papa looked worn and tired beyond his years. The decades of heavy drinking and his numerous accidents and head injuries had taken a toll on his once-hardy frame. It hurt me to see him like that.

About a month later, Valerie Danby-Smith arrived at the Finca as Papa's secretary. Valerie was a young reporter from Ireland whom Papa had met in Madrid and invited to join his entourage in La Feria de San Fermín in Pamplona. Valerie tended to his correspondence and typed manuscripts while Papa worked hard on the mano-a-mano between Dominguín and Ordóñez. Hemingway asked for extensions from *Life,* which had contracted him to write a 30,000-word article, which by the end of May became a 100,000-word draft for a book.

El Trofeo Hemingway fishing contest had been held every month of May since 1950. Papa had helped set up the event. In 1960 the tournament was sponsored by El Instituto Nacional de la Industria Turística, or INIT. It was a well-organized event with fishermen from all over the world participating. The judges for the event consisted of two members of INIT, Jesus Martínez and Baudillo Castillo, and a third judge, American photographer Hy Peskins. Prior to the event this year, the Cuban press confirmed that Fidel Castro would participate in the tournament aboard the yacht *Cristal,* which was owned by the proprietor of the Tropical Beer Brewery, Julio Blanco Herrera. Castro was accompanied by his guards and three Cuban photographers.

For five days the participants went out at their designated time hoping to catch the prize-winning fish. On Sunday, May 15, the silver cup was awarded to Fidel Castro, with Hemingway personally handing over the trophy. It was the only time the two men ever spoke, and the only time they were photographed together.

CUBA 1961

In August of 1960, Hemingway, Mary, and Valerie Danby-Smith traveled to the United States before heading to Spain. As I watched them leave the Finca, I wondered if I would ever see them again.

Papa looked at the house and the ceiba tree as he went down the steps, and I could see sadness wash over him. It was difficult for Papa to leave Cuba thinking that he would never return to his beloved tropical paradise. But the times and the government had changed, and even though he was loved and admired by the Cuban people, there was a great deal of anti-American sentiment on the island. He had also been feeling pressure from U.S. diplomats to leave communist Cuba.

In Spain, Hemingway continued working intensely on *Verano Sangriento* (*The Dangerous Summer*), which took a lot out of him. From La Consula, Mary wrote telling me how nervous and agitated he was. The pressure to fullfill his contractual obligation with *Life* and the amount of information and number of photographs he wanted to gather to finish the book were taking a toll on him. She said she couldn't convince him to go back to the Finca. He felt that he still had a lot of work to do on the book. Their trip back to the States was postponed several times.

After their return to the States in October, Mary wrote telling me that Papa's health and mental state had grown worse. She didn't provide any details, but I knew that she was very concerned. In December he was admitted to the Mayo Clinic in Minnesota. He was released from the clinic only to be readmitted a short time later.

In late June 1961, I received a letter from Papa. The letter began in his sturdy, circular, handsome script and ended in a poor, almost unreadable mess, with the sentences at the end of each line slanting severely downward on the page. I realized from the contents of that letter that he was saying good-bye. I knew he would not return to Cuba and that he was very ill. I memorized every line of that letter and carried it with me until the day I left Cuba. Regrettably, it was lost along with my manuscript and photographs.

> René, mi querido hijo cubano:
> Papa is running out of gas. I don't even have the will to read which was what I loved above everything and writing is even more difficult. I'm very thin. I went from a heavyweight down to a lightheavy and middleweight. Soon I'll be a welterweight like you. The doctors have forbidden salt, fats, and a number of other things. Please look after my cats and dogs and my beloved Finca. Be sure that whatever happens Papa will always remember and take care of you. The manuscripts that you have no matter what happens give them only to Miss Mary.
>
> Abrazos, Papa

On Sunday, July 2nd, I awoke early. I had slept in Mary's room, where I kept a rifle under the bed. I hid another under the sofa in the living room. I didn't want to take any chances with intruding revolucionarios or souvenir thiefs coming to the house. Once Pedrito arrived, I went to see my wife and two sons. I walked down to the gate and headed to my house. At home Fanny was listening to the old Cuban songs station on our portable Zenith radio that Papa had given to me a couple of Christmases before. A special news bulletin interrupted the music and announced that "famous American novelist, Ernest Hemingway, friend of Cuba and the Cuban people, had died earlier in the morning. He suffered a mortal head wound while cleaning his firearm. Ernest Hemingway, recipient of the Nobel Prize for literature, has died."

Three times before I had heard reports of Hemingway's death. The first was during the Second World War when he was presumed dead after a vehicle accident; the second and third were after the plane crashes in Africa. Those times something inside me told me he was still alive. But this time I knew it was for real. Papa's last letter made sense.

He had not been dying from a disease. He had been thinking of killing himself. So many things came to my mind. I remembered when he used to tell friends at the Finca how he would blow his head off with a shotgun by placing it in his mouth and tripping the trigger with his big toe. "This is the way to perform hari-kari with a gun," he would say. I also remembered the "death bet" he had with his longtime friend Gary Cooper, as to who would die first. Cooper died of cancer a couple of months before Hemingway killed himself. I recalled other conversations between Papa and his friends, when he told them that no one would ever see his body at the funeral, that he would not have an open casket. "My face will not be recognizable. I will not allow people to parade in front of me." Perhaps he always knew he would end up like that, or that an accident would take his life. He was a man of action, but I never thought he would take his own life.

In the days after Papa's death, I was upset and confused. The world I had known most of my life had crumbled around me. The security, tranquility, and beauty of the place were gone. The days were filled with anguish and chaos. I was plagued by reporters and phone calls from desperate people trying to obtain details about Papa's death and his life in Cuba. My response was that I had not seen him since he'd left for Spain about a year ago to finish work on *The Dangerous Summer*. I knew how private Papa Hemingway had been his entire life, and I didn't say anything else.

Most of the reporters and biographers were nice, but others were obnoxious, like the two young and hungry vultures—one a writer and the other a filmmaker—who paid me a visit. They came in courteous and friendly, but soon they wanted to know *everything* about Papa. They tried to touch this, grab that. But I wouldn't let them. When I showed them his favorite seat and told them how Papa would only allow a very important guest or friend to sit on it, I had not even finished saying the words before one of them tried to plant his dirty, unworthy ass on it. I grabbed him by the arm and escorted both of them out of the house. "I only wanted to sit on the chair for good luck," the man said to me. I know I made a couple of new enemies, but neither one of them deserved to sit in Papa's chair. Neither one of them was half the man or writer he was. Only over my dead body would they have sat in his chair! It takes a lot more than desire to be a writer to try to fill Hemingway's shoes.

I spent the days thinking about Papa and Mary. I couldn't imagine what she must have been going through. I knew how she loved and cared for him. My thoughts went out to her. Although I had never before felt uncomfortable in the Finca, I wished to be anywhere else. The Finca had always been my paradise and sanctuary. But after Papa's death, the memories, the house, and his room haunted me.

A couple of weeks after Papa's death, Mary telephoned from the United States. After we shared a solemn greeting, there was silence. I was glad to hear her voice, but there was nothing I could say to comfort her.

"René, soon I will travel to Cuba," she said, breaking the awkward silence. "I'll go with Valerie." She then asked how everything was at the Finca. I tried to sound strong in my responses, but my voice eventually broke. "Take it easy," she said, composing her own voice. "We'll talk more once I get there." I heard the click on the other line.

I held the phone in my hand for a long time and thought of the wonderful times we all had together. The happy homecomings from their long trips. The way they loved getting back into their everyday lives. It would never happen again.

A few days later, as I took my walk around the property checking the grounds—there was no reason to hurry—at the entrance to the Finca I saw several black cars parked in front of the gate. I allowed myself to be seen. Someone in one of the cars leaned on the horn several times, trying to get my attention. I walked toward the gate, thinking they were the reporters who had been camped out there since news of Papa's death.

But when the car doors opened, I was surprised to see several officers step out. They approached the gate and motioned for me to come closer. I had no idea what was going on. Then, as I walked toward the gate, I saw Fidel Castro walk to the front of the group. He asked if this was the house of Ernest Hemingway. I said yes. Several armed soldiers got out of the cars.

"Do you know who I am?" he asked, a slight smirk on his face.

"Yes, of course. Fidel Castro, accompanied by his officers."

"Where can we find René Villarreal?"

"I'm René Villarreal."

"You're the man the newspapers say lived next to Hemingway since childhood? Can we come in and talk? We would like to see how he lived." I agreed, not knowing which question I had answered. Castro noticed how nervous I was. "Calm down. There is no need to be nervous. Open the gate so we can come in and talk."

I opened the gate, and Fidel Castro walked in, followed by six other officers, among them Comandante René Vallejo, his friend and personal physician. A group of soldiers followed them in and more soldiers exited the vehicles and stationed themselves outside the gate. The vehicles were driven onto the Finca grounds and the soldiers spread out around the property in groups of two and three.

Behind me I heard the murmur of a crowd of people gathering outside the gate. We turned around and saw a growing multitude on the other side of the gate, even some shouts for Castro. Word had gotten out: Fidel Castro was at the Finca Vigía. The people of the pueblo probably thought El Comandante himself had come to intervenir, to appropriate the property and claim it for the Cuban people. We continued our walk to the house, up the narrow road surrounded on both sides with mango trees, hibiscus, coral vine, and other wild vegetation.

"These mango trees—did Hemingway plant them?" Castro asked.

"No. They were already here when he bought the house. If any got sick or died, he had another planted in the same spot. You see that some are younger than others."

"The hibiscus, other plants, and trees appear to be completely abandoned," he said.

"Ever since Papa Hemingway bought this property, pruning has not been permitted. These paths filled with hibiscus were here from the previous owner, who pruned them, but they never looked this beautiful."

"What do you mean by that?" Castro asked, intrigued.

"We have taken great care of the gardens and trees by employing several gardeners to fumigate, water, and maintain the vegetation. They are charged with keeping the grounds beautiful and healthy, but they are never allowed to prune, not even trim a branch from a tree."

"This is all so interesting," said René Vallejo. "The newspapers say you were his right-hand man, su hombre de confianza. How long did you know him?"

"A little over twenty years. I was just a child when we met after he returned from the Spanish Civil War back in 1939."

We walked around a small bend in the road and came across an old ruin of abandoned brick and plaster. It used to be a cowshed on what was once Don Julian's property. Next to it was a small wooden house with a red Spanish-tile roof. I told them that Don Julian Rodríguez was one of the previous owners of that piece of land. After his death, his wife and children divided the property into several parcels and sold them. Hemingway thought it would be wise to buy some of the land in order to keep the new neighbors as far from the main house as possible. When Hemingway bought that piece of land the ruins were already there. He decided it could serve as a shield for shooting practice. Once the neighbors moved in, he didn't practice there anymore. He was concerned that a stray bullet might accidentally hit one of the new neighbors. I told them he had a cement wall built between the pool and the tennis court, closer to the main house. Arnaldo de la Torre, a mason, bought the leftover materials from the construction of the Carretera Central at a good price from someone in public works, and Hemingway paid him to do the job. I also told them that the Finca was not farmed for profit and that there were eighteen kinds of mango, mamey, guavas, lime trees, peaches, and royal palm trees growing freely all over the property. Fidel Castro looked at his officers and smiled.

When we reached the front of the garage, I pointed out the bungalow and mentioned that Hemingway's sons stayed there when they visited, as well as other long-term visitors. We walked over to the house, up the long steps, and stood under the giant ceiba tree, taking advantage of its shade on this hot July afternoon. Castro walked closer to the ceiba and tapped the massive trunk.

"How can this massive tree survive here with all this concrete around it?" he asked.

"All of this belongs to this great tree, and we must respect it," I said smiling.

"What do you mean by that?"

"Papa admired this tree very much, and sometimes when he walked past it he tapped the trunk. He was amazed by its size and color. He mentioned that the color of the bark reminded him of the skin of the elephants in Africa."

"You still haven't answered my question. What do you mean when you say 'all this belongs to the ceiba tree'?" Castro asked.

I told him that Hemingway used to say that the house was old but that the ceiba tree was older and had grown here by chance of nature. The person who had built the house did not wish to disturb it. He respected the tree. Hemingway knew Cubans believed the ceiba to be a sacred tree and that they should be respected, never cut down. Papa said he could only imagine how sacrilegious it must have been to even consider cutting down a ceiba back in those days. Castro looked at the tree and tapped the trunk. Several officers followed El Comandante's lead.

Castro, the officers, and I then walked to the entrance of the house. One of the officers pointed to the metal bell that hung high on the left column and asked what it was used for. I told him that the bell had been made in 1928 (I had seen the date branded on the inside one day when I cleaned it) and that it was often used when someone arrived unannounced. They would make their presence known by tolling the bell. Sometimes we used it to alert Juan, the chauffeur, if Hemingway or Mary had an unexpected trip. The bell could be heard for some distance. We went inside, and I gave them a tour of the house and then the tower.

Castro said that he had been observing me with great interest. He noted how I spoke about Hemingway's everyday customs, how he worked, details of the house, artwork, hunting trophies, and books. There was never a moment of hesitation on my part on any of their inquiries. He said that the Finca Vigía was a living museum and I was its natural guide. "As soon as la señora Hemingway arrives, I want to speak with her. I'm going to offer to purchase the Finca Vigía and make it a museum. Conserving this place as a museum would be a great tribute to Ernest Hemingway."

I remained quiet. Fidel Castro was clearly excited about this project, but the question remained of how Mary would react. Would she accept the terms of his offer?

Just then two vehicles drove up to the driveway. A soldier from one of the cars stepped out, approached Castro, and pointed out the time. Castro said he had a pending engagement and would have to leave. "Keep maintaining the house as always. I will return to talk more about Hemingway." Castro shook my hand and thanked me. The rest of the officers followed with the same courtesy and then walked down the steps, got into the cars, and left.

I thought about what Fidel Castro had said and walked over to the ceiba tree. Deep down I had a feeling something terrible was going to happen to the ceiba and the Finca as well. I stroked the massive trunk of the tree.

"My dear ceiba. How many times I have sat under your shade to collect my thoughts and rest," I said out loud, now sitting on one of the large roots. "I have wonderful memories in this place and of my life with Papa and Mary. But everything is going to change. No one is going to look after you as Papa did." Tears filled my eyes. I stood up and went inside the house. I smiled to myself and thought, "The tour is officially over. If you have any questions, please don't hesitate to ask." Life is strange. One day you're Ernest Hemingway's hombre de confianza, and the next day Fidel Castro offers you a position as a museum tour guide.

For the rest of the afternoon my thoughts were preoccupied with Castro's visit and all he had said. At nightfall my friend Negrito came up from the pueblo with my adopted brother, David. We sat outside on the front steps of the house close to the ceiba tree. They said the crowd was still outside the entrance gate eagerly waiting to learn more about Castro's visit. I usually went home to have dinner with my wife and spend time with my sons, but the thought of facing all those people made me reconsider. I was tired of answering questions. I was hungry and mentally and physically exhausted. I asked Negrito to bring me dinner from home. David went inside the house to prepare drinks. I wouldn't see my wife or play with my sons that evening.

The news of Fidel Castro's interest in purchasing the Finca Vigía had spread like wildfire through San Francisco de Paula and the city of Havana. Days passed and more reporters and writers arrived at the Finca. Most of them were foreigners. They were very respectful, courteous admirers of Papa Hemingway.

I filled my days working around the house trying not to think of what was going to happen. In the evenings I asked Fanny to bring the boys when she came up with my dinner. I couldn't leave the house alone anymore. I had to stay and guard it constantly. There would be thieves or people that simply wanted a souvenir from the Finca Vigía. Late at night, after my wife and sons left, I lay on the floor of the living room thinking of the old and good times. I waited for Mary to come. Things would be better once she came, I thought.

MARY, AGAIN

Miss Mary arrived in Cuba at the end of July 1961, accompanied by Valerie Danby-Smith. Mary looked thin and sad. We hugged and tried to maintain our composure, bracing ourselves for the tasks ahead.

Several of Papa's old friends came to greet her—Mayito Menocal, Elicio Argüelles, and José Luis and Roberto Herrera. After they left, she got down to business and requested a meeting with Fidel Castro. She drafted a detailed list of what she planned to leave behind, making it clear that what she was leaving behind was for the Cuban people and not for the Cuban government. In her document she also requested to be allowed to take her most valuable and personal possessions out of the country.

Fidel Castro met with Mary at the Finca. She explained her wishes to donate the house to the Cuban people in exchange for being permitted to take the remaining artwork and valuables out of the country. Castro told her that he had to think it over, because the artwork was now patrimonio nacional; it belonged to the Cuban government. He left without giving her a response.

In my possession I had a leather valise stuffed with a manuscript Papa Hemingway had given me for safekeeping. I kept it hidden on the top shelf of his study closet. The manuscript, to which he often referred and to which he added pages throughout the years, was wrapped in a plastic bag, to keep the moisture out, and then in a towel. As per Papa's instructions in his last letter to me, I handed over the valise to Mary. She smiled and hugged me when she opened it and realized what was in it. I didn't know what manuscript it was, but I know Papa had worked on it for many years. There were other manuscripts in safe deposit boxes in a Havana bank that she was also able to retrieve.

Over the next couple of days, Mary carried out her secret agenda with help from me and Valerie. She went through photographs, letters, and magazines from the library and through boxes that were stored in the basement. Once the selections were made, she called me into the library. "We have to destroy all of this," she said. "It was Papa's wish. It all has to be destroyed quickly and quietly." I told her that a bonfire should take care of it. "I want you personally to handle it. No one else. Tu siempre has sido nuestro hombre de confianza," she said looking into my eyes.

I went behind the abandoned cowshed where we burned the garbage from the house and lit the fire. It burned strong fast. I brought a wheelbarrow around the terrace to the French doors of the library.

"This is the most important box. Burn it first," she said nervously. Mary accompanied me to the bonfire. I tossed the box in and watched as the flames consumed the papers. Eventually the box crumbled. I saw relief on Mary's face. "Wait until it all burns, then we'll get the rest," she said, not taking her eyes off the flames.

When we went back for more boxes, she told me that now it was all right to call Pedrito and ask for his assistance. "I'll be in the library with Valerie sorting things out. You stay with the fire and have Pedrito bring the boxes to you," she instructed.

I got Pedrito from the pantry, where he had been waiting until we needed him. He wheeled the boxes to the fire. I threw the boxes in and watched as the fire slowly consumed the photographs, letters, and paperwork. Mary came down with the last wheelbarrow full of boxes and on the way they met Pichilo. Pedrito and Pichilo asked for some photographs to remember Papa by. Mary told them that she would leave several with me and I would distribute them later.

"Do you want to go back to the States with me?" she asked me.

"No, not for now," I said. "I don't want to leave my mother and father behind. I'm still getting over all this. Once you leave, things are going to be different."

"Yes, I'll be far away, but we'll always be in touch," she said.

"I have a letter from Papa," I told her, taking the letter out of the breast pocket of my guayabera and handing it to her. She read the letter and wept. She carefully folded it and gave it back to me.

"Keep it," she said, wiping the tears from her face. "Hold on to it. One of his wishes was to never publish his letters."

"I have a lot more letters from both of you. You want me to toss them into the fire?"

"No, those are yours. Save them." She also said that she wanted to give me several articles of clothing and shoes that belonged to Papa. She planned to give Juan the stationwagon, José Luis the Buick, and Roberto the Chrysler. Gregorio was to keep the *Pilar,* and the cows would go to Pichilo.

"In my room I have the .22 caliber rifle Papa gave me," I said. She told me she'd take care of all the paperwork to make sure everyone knows it belonged to me. She walked back to the house.

The next day, after Mary had gone to the bank in Havana with Juan, she handed each member of the staff an envelope and said that Papa had wanted to give us a token of his appreciation. That afternoon she invited the musical trio from El Floridita to come and play at the house, and afterward she gave them her Spanish guitar as a gift.

The Cuban Ministry of Culture finally agreed to Mary's request and allowed her to take the artwork and personal mementos. Personnel from the conservation branch of one of the art museums was sent to the Finca to build crates and pack up the items Mary was to take back with her to the States. The Ministry also said that all employees could stay on working in the house. But Pichilo, Pedrito, and I planned on leaving. After twenty years of working for Papa Hemingway, I felt I couldn't stay. The place brought back too many memories, and nothing was going to be the same ever again.

The night before Mary was to leave, we talked in the living room.

"I always thought you would stay at the Finca," she said. "Now I realize that when I leave you'll leave right behind me. Papa and I always thought of leaving this house for you and your family."

"I thought we would always be together," I said.

"I know. We had good times here."

That evening she told me that whenever I wanted out of Cuba, she would take care of it.

On the morning of August 27, 1961, Mary and Valerie walked out of the house, and I followed them. Juan was waiting for them in the driveway with the stationwagon. I hugged and kissed Mary and held her tight. She looked at me and started to cry. Mary and Valerie got to the stationwagon, waved, and drove away. I walked to the garage, where there was a jeep with four milicianos and an officer waiting for me. I walked back to the house with them and introduced them to Ana Tsar, the laundress, who was staying as head of the staff. I showed them how to secure the house. When I closed the last window, I felt as if I had closed a chapter in my life.

Two of the milicianos stayed up by the house and took quarters in the basement. The other two drove me down to the gate and stationed themselves, posting guard. I walked to the Carretera Central, turned left until I reached Diego Franchi, my street, and went home.

PARADISE LOST

Not a week had passed before Ana came to my house in a frantic state. "They've killed all the cats!" she screamed in horror. She told me that jovenes rebeldes (revolutionary youths) had relieved los milicianos from their posts at the Finca. Los milicianos had guarded and maintained the house well, but the jovenes rebeldes were different. They were uneducated young men who only recently had been given authority and power. They had police dogs with them and went to the tower, and there the dogs killed the cats.

I was furious and wanted to go to the Finca and confront them. But there was nothing I could do. After leaving the Finca, I was forbidden from entering the grounds. I told her to speak to Roberto Herrera in Havana. A couple of days later she came back even more depressed. I could tell she had been crying for days. Roberto had told her "el muerto al hoyo y el vivo al poyo"—the dead to the hole and the living to the fowl. It loses the flavor in the translation, but what he told her was that he simply didn't give a shit.

A few days later, with the excuse of visiting my adopted brother, David, I walked past the Finca on my way to his house. David told me more jovenes rebeldes had arrived and were all over the house. They had brought heavy artillery and were taking target practice on the trees. I hated them all without personally knowing any one of them.

Three months after leaving the Finca, Pichilo and Pedrito found employment. However, the position that had been promised to me in the Hatuey beer brewery never materialized. I went for over three months without a job. Money was not a problem, since I had the money Papa had left me. Finally, in December, I found employment in El Cotorro at a steel mill, La Antillana de Acero. My brother Luis left his job with the water company and started to work with me in the processing line. It was hard work, but we soon got used to it.

Late in 1962, Fidel Castro visited the Finca Vigía once more, this time accompanied by the captain of the *African Paylor,* a ship that carried medicine and supplies in exchange for prisoners from the failed Bay of Pigs invasion. The captain was a big fan of Hemingway's work and wished to visit the Finca Vigía. Earlier that day, on a visit to David, I had seen several vehicles and more guards than usual by the gate of the Finca. I wondered what all the commotion was about. Not long into our visit, there was a knock on the door. An alarmed David returned and told me there were two armed milicianos asking for me. I had a clear conscience and had nothing to worry about. Calmly, I went to find out what they wanted. Los milicianos ordered me to accompany them into the jeep.

I expected a long ride somewhere to a military station, but instead the jeep drove around the corner and stopped in front of the Finca's gate. Once inside the property, the jeep turned up the incline road. I could see Fidel Castro and another man waiting by the steps of the house. As soon as I got out of the jeep, Castro shook my hand and introduced me to the captain of the *African Paylor*.

"You didn't want to stay. You left and look what they have done." Castro was upset. He remembered how the house looked the first time he visited, but the jovenes rebeldes had fired their guns inside the house and there were bullet holes in the walls. There were also several trees riddled with more holes. And the dogs had torn the Philippine matting in the living room. Castro then asked me to show the captain the most important aspects of the house.

After the tour, Castro was even more upset at the state of the house. He asked me to return to the Finca as director and administrator. He wanted me to restore it to the way it was. "Make-believe Hemingway is still alive," he said. "You'll have final word on everything. Come back tomorrow." He said that first thing tomorrow morning there would be personnel waiting for me at the Finca to begin the restoration process.

He asked me what I needed or wanted from him. I said in a low voice, "I want all the police dogs out, and I don't want to see any jovenes rebeldes around here."

"They're already out, and they're going to pay for this!" El Comandante said, his voice raised.

The Hemingway Museum was assigned to El Consejo Nacional de Cultura, the National Council of Culture. Carlos Lechuga was its head, and a man I simply knew as Señor Ascue was his second in command. They were both fine gentlemen and scholars and assisted me in securing any material and personnel I requested.

At the end of 1962, I returned to my paradise—my destroyed paradise. In a matter of days I had met with interior designers, carpenters, and landscapers. It would take months to return the grounds and property to the way it had been. Everything had to be restored. While there were significant funds available for all the restoration, there was no one to restore the Philippine matting. At that time David needed money, since he had been out of work for a short time, so I contracted him for that job and secretly helped him restore the matting in the living room.

Roberto Herrera and Fernando Campoamor secured cushy jobs at the Finca. Roberto insisted that he had been Hemingway's personal secretary and was given the position of conservator of the museum. Fernando was given the title of "attaché of foreign public relations." The men came in once or twice a month and walked around with the delegations and mingled with the visitors.

What I really needed was personnel to assist me in maintaining the house, not freeloaders with made-up jobs. Ana and I did all the maintenance work in the house. I worked six days a week, resting only on Tuesday.

One day Gregorio Fuentes visited the museum. He wanted a job. He was going through hard times. He had been unable to maintain the *Pilar* with all the expensive repairs and had to turn it in to the government. He wanted a smaller boat so he could join the cooperative of fishermen from Cojímar. I told him to speak with Carlos Lechuga from the ministry. Not long after that the *Pilar* was brought to the Finca for the first time. The yacht didn't fit through the front gate, so we had to knock down a stretch of fence on the side of the property. Then more extensive maintanance work had to be done, and it was transported to Cárdenas for several months. The *Pilar* was eventually returned to the Finca and placed close to the pool.

El Museo Ernest Hemingway en Cuba was inaugurated in July 1963. A few months later, El Consejo Nacional de Cultura transferred the responsibilities of the museums in Havana to El Palacio de Bellas Artes, which was under the direction of Marta Arjona. From the beginning, Marta Arjona and I had difficulties. She couldn't understand how someone holding such an important position as administrator, director, and guide of the Hemingway Museum was not, or had never been, an active participant in political gatherings or had ever shown a hint of support for the revolution. My apolitical status was not acceptable to her, and neither was my level of education. Eventually she started making things difficult for me by holding back supplies necessary for maintaining the museum. And when I requested more trained personnel due to the growing number of visitors and important delegations, instead she sent inexperienced individuals.

She tried all she could to get me to quit. One afternoon she sent a young man who had been given the title of "head administrator of the Hemingway Museum." It never occurred to the poor young man that he was being sent to the slaughterhouse. After he introduced himself, I asked him a few questions. I realized that he had never read one thing written by Ernest Hemingway. He had never met Hemingway and had never visited the Finca Vigía before. Yet he was sent as "head administrator" to order me around. I sent him back to Havana that same day. Insulted, Marta Arjona demanded an audience with me. Instead, I went directly to her superiors and explained my situation. She got off my case for a while.

In 1963, in a social experiment by the new regime, all the museums closed at a national level. El Consejo Nacional de Cultura requested volunteers from each museum to assist in the tobacco plantations for a month. One of my assistants, Gerardo Muñoz, and I represented the museum. We were the only young and strong available men working at the Finca at the time.

A short while later I was recruited to train to defend Cuba against foreign invaders. With other men from San Francisco de Paula, I went to a training camp in Mantilla two nights a week after work. There we were instructed on the arming and disarming of antiaircraft artillery, among other things. A couple of months later, after the training was completed, and without much warning, they recruited us again for another three weeks of combat training somewhere else. During the first week of training, an important Soviet delegation visiting Cuba was interested in seeing the temporarily closed Ernest Hemingway Museum. When the delegation had to be sent away, embarrassing several people in high goverment positions, I was sent back to the museum immediately and given active reserve status. "René Villarreal was not to be bothered unless the country was under attack" were the orders from high up in the diplomatic council. That made me happy.

It was a surreal existence: one day I guide a foreign delegation through the Hemingway Museum and the next day I'm called to arm and disarm antiaircraft artillery or pick tobacco. Those extreme situations gave me reasons for concern and forced me to reconsider my family's future in Cuba.

EXPULSION FROM PARADISE

By the late 1960s, I was a thorn firmly planted in Marta Arjona's side. One day, without much warning, I received a phone call from her office. The unidentified person on the other end of the line informed me that an important foreign diplomatic delegation was scheduled to visit the Hemingway Museum. That same person suggested I should receive the delegation wearing a miliciano uniform. I told them that I had no uniform and that El Consejo Nacional de Cultura had never issued uniforms of any kind to the museum staff. I went on to say that during all the years I worked at the Finca, I wore guayaberas and dress slacks, and I wasn't planning to wear anything else. Needless to say, the irritated person slammed the receiver down hard.

A couple of days later I received another telephone call from El Palacio de Bellas Artes informing me that another important delegation would be arriving at the museum. It was a delegation of foreign war heroes and their wives. I was instructed to close the museum to the general public and attend only to them. They also wanted people who had firsthand knowledge of Hemingway's life in Cuba to be present and ready to answer questions. The only other person available on such short notice was Gregorio Fuentes. Gregorio had been able to receive a smaller boat in exchange for the *Pilar* and had joined the cooperativa de pescadores. But because of his old age, he had had to give up fishing. Fortunately, I was able to get him a permanent position at the Finca.

When the delegation arrived, I began the tour outside of the house. When we reached the dining room area, I allowed them to come into the house. In addition to the delegation's escort, who spoke Russian to the visitors, I had the help of my two assistants, Gregorio Fuentes, and the two milicianos who guarded the museum at night. At one point, as I turned my back to the group to point out one of the trophies on the west wall of the dining room, I saw out of the corner of my eye one of the female visitors take a dessert spoon from the table and put it in her bag. The silverware displayed on the table was the expensive silverware Mary had brought back from Venice with Hemingway's emblem engraved on it. My two assistants witnessed it too, as did Gregorio, the other members of the delegation, and the escort. The two milicianos looked at me and confirmed that they had also witnessed it. Discreetly, I approached the escort. He said to wait until the tour was over and he would speak to the woman.

The woman knew we had seen her. Nervous, she insisted on going out to the terrace. I whispered to Gregorio to follow her. He followed her as she walked toward the tour bus. I quietly urged the escort to do something before she got the opportunity to discard the evidence.

"Compañero, you're accusing one of the wives of these distinguished officers of theft!?" he said in a loud voice, capturing everyone's attention and expecting me to back down and not confront him. But I confronted him and demanded that the silver spoon be returned.

The infuriated man turned to the delegation and spoke to them. By the reaction of the group and the tone of his voice, I knew it was not good. "I told them you said they were all thieves!" I gestured "no" to the delegation and then, clenching my fist in his face, demanded that the guide tell them the truth.

"You're mierda now! You'll end up in jail or working in the fields!" he blurted.

I held back. Things were bad already, and if I hit him it would get worse.

"Let's call Fidel Castro right now," I said. "Let him hear both sides of the story. When this is over, then let's see who's going to jail. Or, if you want, we can settle it como hombres!"

"I'm an officer. I'm not a common street brawler," the man said nervously.

"Lo que no tienes son cojones!" I said, my jaw clenched.

The rest of the delegation watched the altercation in astonishment. There was no way I could communicate to them and explain and let them know I had never called them thieves. Fortunately, my assistants backed me up. A day later the missing spoon was found in the woman's hotel room among other items from different museums. It turns out she was a kleptomaniac.

After that episode, one of my assistants confessed to me that she was an undercover agent working for the state. She had been sent to work at the Finca and spy on me and find out if I was involved in any contrarevolutionary activity. She told me that she had nothing but respect and admiration for me and had informed her superiors that all I did was work and maintain the museum. She told them that I worked between the tours cleaning and fixing and managing the museum with the little supplies I was given. I was pleased to hear this, but I was not surprised. From the day she started working in the Finca, I knew she was seguridad. A friend in high places had warned me.

In 1967 Marta Arjona kept sending more people for me to train. I knew eventually one of them would replace me. It was part of her plan. She was making my life impossible. My stubborness didn't help matters either. I didn't care about government or its rules. I just wanted to keep Papa Hemingway's memory alive. I was offended when Marta Arjona said I should be proud of being so privileged because Fidel Castro himself had requested me for the job. I responded by saying that I had been privileged knowing Papa Hemingway.

By 1968 my situation at the museum had become unbearable. No one dared get rid of me since Castro himself had appointed me director. I saw no sign of hope. I was not going to give in to their regulations and demands to attend endless meetings, to having to maintain the museum with little or no supplies, and to being constantly spied on. I realized I wanted out of the Finca and out of Cuba.

One afternoon in late June of 1968, I happened to see a couple standing by the Finca gate. From the moment I saw Enrique Cervantes I realized that he was an honest, good-hearted person. He was accompanied by his wife's aunt, who lived in New York City and was visiting Havana. I told them to come back the next day and I would give them a private tour. The next day Enrique came with his wife, Marta, and her aunt. After that we met a couple more times.

I asked Enrique to get a confidential letter to Mary Hemingway through his aunt. In the letter I asked Miss Mary to get me and my family out. My mother had died in 1964 from heart disease, and my father had given me his blessing to leave the country. A month later, Mary wrote back and told me to count on her for whatever I needed.

I had to resign in person in El Palacio de Bellas Artes. An ecstatic and joyful Marta Arjona forbade me to set foot inside the Finca. Once again I found myself expelled from my paradise. But I had to do it, and I had the satisfaction of having restored the Finca and rescuing it away from the insolent jovenes rebeldes who had nearly destroyed it and massacred the cats. I knew the Finca Vigía would remain as a remembrance of Papa Hemingway's legacy in Cuba.

In 1969 I was sentenced to two years of hard labor cutting sugar cane in Oriente—a mandatory service you had to provide for your country if you wanted to leave. The other men in the camps were just like me—honest people who just wanted to leave Cuba. Men who were tired of the government's oppression and injustices, we were sent to work under inhumane conditions doing a job we knew nothing about. We worked twelve hours a day for one peso a day. But we did it. We endured the hard work, the hunger, the hardships. We endured being treated like common criminals. We did it for our families. We also did it for ourselves and to prove they would never break us.

It was also hard for my family back in San Francisco de Paula. No matter how well my children did in school, their efforts were never acknowledged. They didn't matter to the school system since we weren't revolucionarios. It was very difficult for my brothers and sister, too, because they were expected to disown me. But that's where the system failed. Blood is blood. My sister and brothers never turned their backs on me.

My father passed away in 1971, which freed me to leave the country. After my term of hard labor was complete, and with Miss Mary having taken care of all the travel expenses, on March 12, 1972, Fanny, my five children, and I left Cuba and flew to Spain.

Kid Tunero and other friends met us at the Madrid airport. Enrique Cervantes and his wife offered us their home. I had met him only briefly a few times when he visited the museum, yet now he offered me his home as a brother would do. We became great friends. The friendship between our children also grew, and to this day they refer to each other as cousins. Shortly after arriving in Madrid we found an apartment in the same area the Cervantes family lived. Mary helped by sending money every month. I found a job hauling scrap metal and told her that she did not have to help anymore. But she insisted on it. She had always been a darling to me. From the first day I met her she had treated me like a son.

In 1973 the Cervantes family moved to the United States and settled in Virginia. Enrique wrote and told me how well they were adapting to life in America and the great employment opportunities there. So in 1974 my family migrated to the United States and settled in New Jersey, where I have lived ever since. Immediately after our arrival, I found a custodial job at Sears Roebuck & Company, very close to where we lived in Union City. Some months later I switched to a better job in New York City at a ring factory, also doing custodial work. I worked as much overtime as possible to support my family. When the owner of the factory found out that I had worked for Ernest Hemingway, he gave me the opportunity to learn to Swiss-cut wedding rings. It was a better paying job with health benefits. I worked there until my retirement.

In 1973, in Spain, I gave my last interview about my life with Ernest Hemingway. It wasn't until 1999 that I agreed to be interviewed again. During the intervening years I was silent. Numerous reporters and biographers were interested in interviewing me, but I simply declined. I did not feel like telling my story then.

I've lived an interesting life, and now I'm happy to be telling my story. I've read numerous biographies of Hemingway—many I liked but others I hated for their discrepancies and lies. I know there were people who saw me only as Hemingway's faithful servant. Perhaps that was all they wanted to see. It was difficult for them to understand why a man like Ernest Hemingway placed so much trust in me. They were the ones who were never able to reach him because he refused to have anything to do with them. They needed to create a false image of the man because they didn't have any point of reference. They spoke ill of him simply because he ignored them.

The Hemingway I knew was a simple man—a man who respected the truth, embraced simplicity and honesty. He was a man who would rather dine and drink with fishermen, boxers, ballplayers, and common folk than with writers or intellectuals. "You're only asking for trouble if you do," he often said about consorting with other writers. He was a man who disliked the ambitious and opportunistic, leeches and vultures. That was the reason why he chose not to meet with certain people, and I know that was the reason he confided in me. He knew that I, too, valued honesty.

No person is without faults. And certainly Ernest Hemingway was no exception. But as many faults as he had, he also possessed many great virtues. And I was lucky enough to have witnessed, experienced them. Whatever demons Papa faced each morning when he stepped in front of the mirror, they were his and only his. And when he could no longer do what he did best and loved the most, he took his own life. On that Sunday morning, July 2, 1961, Papa Hemingway shot his last lion.

IN DREAMS

I walked down the steps from the terrace that led to the pool and saw Papa Hemingway swimming. He swam a breaststroke, exercising his powerful arms and chest. He saw me and waved me over. I walked over to the edge of the pool, squatted down, and waited for him to reach me.

"How's your swimming?" he asked.

"Not that good," I said.

"Why? You know how to swim?"

"It's hard for me now," I told him.

"It's easy."

"It's easy if you know how to do it," I smiled.

He touched my edge of the pool and turned. "No. It's easy. You just have to take your time," he said, slowly moving away with strong, steady strokes. He reached the other end of the pool, touched the edge, and headed back to me. He didn't tire. He swam, keeping the same pace.

"You make it look easy. You're a natural," I said. "But believe me, it's hard."

"No te apures," he said, continuing with his slow and easy breaststroke. "Take your time and relax." He parted the water with his hands, pushing forward, reaching my edge, touching it, and turning. He reached the other edge and turned back. He took his time with each stroke and kick.

"When you get tired, take a rest. Give yourself time to think about what you're doing. It will come easy." He slowed down in the middle of the pool. He looked up and smiled.

"You're a natural, a great swimmer," I said.

"Some are born good swimmers, others not. All you can do is try," he said, still smiling at me.

"It's just very difficult for me now. I'm not a natural."

"Suave. The more you do it, the easier it gets."

"You just make it look very easy."

"I was born a swimmer. I've had lots of practice." He turned. He reached the middle of the pool, looked back at me, waved, and continued swimming freestyle, moving faster.

I stood up and thought about what he had said. Turning to go up to the house, I looked up to the sky.

Then I woke up.

It had been a dream.

I got out of bed, looked at the clock. It was not even 6:00 A.M. "It's hard for an old man to sleep late," I said to myself. Then I went to the kitchen table with my clipboard, pencils, and paper to write.